acts

D0844090

the

acts

of the apostles

authorised king james version

printed by authority

published by canongate

with an introduction by │ p d james

First published in Great Britain in 1999
by Canongate Books Ltd
14 High Street, Edinburgh EH1 1TE

10 9 8 7 6 5 4 3 2 1

Introduction copyright © PD James 1999
The moral right of the author has been asserted

British Library Cataloguing-in-Publication Data
A catalogue record is available on request from
the British Library

ISBN 0 86241 973 5

Typeset by Palimpsest Book Production
Book design by Paddy Cramsie at et al
Printed and bound in Great Britain
by Caledonian International, Bishopbriggs

*LICENCE: In terms of the Letters Patent granted by Her late Majesty Queen Victoria
to Her Printers for Scotland and of the Instructions issued by Her said Majesty in
Council, dated Eleventh July Eighteen Hundred and Thirty nine, I hereby License and
Authorise Canongate Books Limited, Fourteen High Street, Edinburgh, to Print and
Publish, as by the Authority of Her Majesty Queen Elizabeth the Second, but so far
as regards the Text of the Authorised Version only, an Edition of the Acts of the
Apostles in Palatino Type as proposed in their Declaration dated the Twenty first day of
September Nineteen Hundred and Ninety nine.*

Dated at Edinburgh the Twenty eighth day of September Nineteen Hundred and Ninety nine.

HARDIE, Lord Advocate

a note about pocket canons

The Authorised King James Version of the Bible, translated between 1603–11, coincided with an extraordinary flowering of English literature. This version, more than any other, and possibly more than any other work in history, has had an influence in shaping the language we speak and write today.

Twenty-four of the eighty original books of the King James Bible are brought to you in this series. They encompass categories as diverse as history, philosophy, law, poetry and fiction. Each Pocket Canon also has its own introduction, specially commissioned from an impressive range of writers, to provide a personal interpretation of the text and explore its contemporary relevance.

introduction by p d james

P.D. James has won many awards for crime-writing from Britain, America, Italy and Scandinavia, and has received honorary degrees from six universities. In 1983 she received the OBE and in 1991 she was created a life peer. Her novels include An Unsuitable Job for a Woman, Innocent Blood, Shroud for a Nightingale, A Taste for Death, The Children of Men, Original Sin *and* A Certain Justice. *She lives in London.*

No book of the New Testament has a plainer and less ambiguous title than has the fifth, *The Acts of the Apostles*, but it is hardly an accurate description of this complex, fascinating and occasionally puzzling testimony in which the majority of the Apostles are only briefly named. To read *Acts* is to be drawn into a world of dramatic incident thronged with characters from all walks of life, a world of many nations and tongues; Parthians and Medes, Elamites, Cretes and Arabians, some of whom briefly appear and then as mysteriously disappear. This personal account of the formative years of the Christian Church is dominated by two very different characters, both of immense stature and importance: Peter, the rock on which Christ said He would build His Church, and Paul of Tarsus, the religious genius who, following his dramatic conversion, carried the new faith to the Gentile world and formulated its theology.

The story opens with the command of Jesus that His disciples should wait in Jerusalem for the promised baptism with the Holy Ghost, after which they would be empowered to be witnesses to Him, 'both in Jerusalem and in all Judaea, and in Samaria, and unto the uttermost part of the earth' (1:8). By the end of the book we have seen this promise fulfilled. By the power of the Holy Spirit the faith has spread like sparks from a fire, leaping from community to community through the Mediterranean world until it reaches the gates of Rome itself.

From the end of the second century the tradition of the Church has ascribed authorship of *Acts* to Luke, who wrote the first gospel. Both works are dedicated to Theophilus. The style and vocabulary of both are consistent with the same authorship and it would seem that the two books were intended to be read as one narrative. Luke is mentioned only three times in the New Testament, all in the letters of Paul. In *Colossians* 4:14 he writes: 'Luke, the beloved physician, and Demas, greet you'. When writing to Philemon he refers to Luke as one of his fellow workers, and in the fourth chapter of the second letter to Timothy, he writes: 'Only Luke is with me'(4:11). It does seem likely that Luke accompanied Paul on some of his journeys, particularly since sections in the second half of the book changed from the third-person to the first-person narrative, and are obviously a personal account. But it is extraordinary that we know so little of the man who, through his writing, was so influential in the life of the Church.

We know even less of the dedicatee Theophilus. Luke, in his gospel, gave him the title 'Excellency'. Was he a provincial governor or other powerful man drawn to the new religion but waiting to be convinced of its truth before accepting baptism? Was he even a real person? But he certainly stands for the very many people whom Luke was addressing and seeking to convince and convert by this extraordinary, richly-populated and complex mixture of religious apologia, adventure story and travelogue. *Acts* was probably written about 60 AD, although some authorities date it twenty years later. If 60 AD is roughly correct, then Luke may well have spoken to witnesses who actually met Jesus during His ministry.

The most dramatic and arguably the most important episode in *Acts*, apart from Christ's ascension and the coming of the Holy Spirit, is the conversion of Paul, then called Saul. He was an indefatigable persecutor of the Way and had been present at the stoning to death of Stephen, the first martyr. Now 'breathing out threatenings and slaughter against the disciples of the Lord'(9:1), he obtained from the high priest letters to the synagogue at Damascus authorising him to bring in men or women followers of the Way bound for Jerusalem.

While he was on the road and coming close to Damascus, there was a sudden light from Heaven shining around him. He fell to the ground and heard a voice saying: 'Saul, Saul, why persecutest thou me?' Trembling and astonished he asked, 'Lord, what wilt thou have me to do?(9:6)' He was told to rise and go into the city and there wait to be told what would happen next. The men who were journeying with him stood speechless with amazement, hearing a voice but seeing no-one. When Saul got up from the earth he was blind and his companions had to lead him by the hand and take him into Damascus. There, after three days without sight and without food or drink, the disciple named Ananias came to him, restored his sight, confirmed to him that the Lord had indeed appeared to him on the way, and baptised him. In that extraordinary moment of revelation on the Damascus road Paul's life was irrevocably changed and the history of the Western world was set on a different course.

It would not, of course, be accurate to think of Paul's conversion in our present sense of the word; he did not abjure his old religion. He and the disciples remained Jews and, when they worshipped, did so in the synagogue. And when they preached the message of Christ crucified and risen, they could not possibly have envisaged that this new religion would spread to lands then undiscovered, or that Jesus of Nazareth would still be worshipped two thousand years after their deaths. They must, indeed, have been in expectation of Christ's early Second Coming.

No organisation with which human beings are concerned, even one divinely ordained or inspired, is ever free from controversy. The main problem facing the new Church was whether Christ's revelation was to the Jews alone or whether Gentiles could also receive the gift of the Spirit and be baptised. The decision, like many others, was preceded by a divine revelation following prayer. Peter, who was at

Joppa, went up on the roof to pray. He was hungry and, while food was being prepared, he fell into a trance. He saw Heaven opening and a great sheet, knotted by its four corners, descend and ascend three times, containing all manner of 'four-footed beasts of the earth, and wild beasts, and creeping things, and fowls of the air'(10:12). Peter heard a voice saying: 'Rise, Peter; kill and eat', but he replied, 'Not so, Lord, for I have never eaten any thing that is common or unclean.' Then the voice spoke to him again: 'What God has cleansed, that call not thou common'(10:13-15). Peter perceived that God is no respecter of persons; the new dispensation of love was to be taken to the whole world.

Inevitably this decision gave rise to further dissension; was it necessary for converts who were not Jews to be circumcised before they were received into the Church? It was decided that the Gentiles must be required to keep the Jewish dietary rules and abstain from fornication, but that they need not be circumcised. The decision was certainly not unanimous and was probably more controversial than Luke admits. It was, however, one more vital step on the journey of Christianity towards world acceptance.

Another decision which caused difficulty arose from the practice of the Church that possessions should be held in common and that distribution should be made according to need. A certain man named Ananias (the second of that name in *Acts*), with Sapphira his wife, sold their possessions, as they were required to do, but kept back part of the price. When Ananais laid the remainder at the apostles' feet, Peter asked Ananias: 'Why has Satan filled thine heart to lie to the

Holy Ghost and to keep back part of the price of the land?(5:3)' On hearing Peter's words, Ananias fell down dead. About three hours later, his wife, not knowing what had happened, came in and received the same question from Peter. She too fell down dead at his feet and was carried out. 'And great fear came upon all the church, and upon as many as heard these things'(5:11). I have always found this a disturbing story and can't help feeling some sympathy for Ananias and his wife. They probably felt it was prudent and not unreasonable, having sold all their possessions, to retain at least part of the proceeds; their punishment – since that is how it is presented in *Acts* – seems more typical of a vengeful Jehovah than of the God of love and forgiveness.

Acts is a restless book, full of comings and going, of dramatic incidents and violent events. We accompany Paul on his three great perilous journeys, but he is not the only traveller; almost all the characters are on the road, healing, raising the dead, preaching, defending themselves before the councils of the great, both in state and synagogue. Luke observes the dramatic events with the eye of a physician and describes them with the discriminating skill of a novelist, providing the human details which add verisimilitude and reinforce the story's humanity and universality.

An example is the release of Paul and Silas from prison in chapter 16, when a great earthquake at midnight shook the prison foundations and opened all the doors. The keeper of the prison, assuming that all his prisoners had fled, drew out his sword to commit suicide, but Paul cried with a loud voice, saying: 'Do thyself no harm for we are all here'(16:28).

Then the keeper called for a light and, falling down before Paul and Silas, asked what he must do to be saved. They said: 'Believe on the Lord Jesus Christ, and thou shalt be saved, and thy house'(16:31). That same night he took them home, washed their weals from the flogging and he and all his family were baptised. The next morning the magistrates sent the serjeants to free Paul and Silas. Paul, however, insisted that the magistrates come in person to do the job, saying that he and Silas had been beaten and imprisoned without having been condemned, despite the fact that they were Roman citizens. Small wonder that, hearing the prisoners were Romans, the magistrates came themselves and exhorted them to leave the city.

The final chapter of *Acts*, chapter 28, ends so suddenly that one wonders whether Luke intended to continue writing. We are left uncertain of Paul's future; the last two sentences merely say that he dwelt for two whole years at Rome in his hired house and received 'all that came in unto him. Preaching the kingdom of God, and teaching those things which concern the Lord Jesus Christ, with all confidence, no man forbidding him'(28:31). The Holy Spirit which had descended upon the disciples in Jerusalem had led the Church to the heart of the Roman Empire. Although Luke's account of Paul's life and ministry ends so abruptly, tradition has it that he was executed in Rome in AD 64–5, under Nero's persecution. The path on which he had set out after that dramatic encounter on the Damascus road, and which he had followed so faithfully, led him at last to a martyr's crown.

p d james

the acts of the apostles

The former treatise have I made, O Theophilus, of all that Jesus began both to do and teach, ² until the day in which he was taken up, after that he through the Holy Ghost had given commandments unto the apostles whom he had chosen: ³ to whom also he shewed himself alive after his passion by many infallible proofs, being seen of them forty days, and speaking of the things pertaining to the kingdom of God; ⁴ and, being assembled together with them, commanded them that they should not depart from Jerusalem, but wait for the promise of the Father, which, saith he, ye have heard of me. ⁵ For John truly baptized with water; but ye shall be baptized with the Holy Ghost not many days hence. ⁶ When they therefore were come together, they asked of him, saying, 'Lord, wilt thou at this time restore again the kingdom to Israel?' ⁷ And he said unto them, 'It is not for you to know the times or the seasons, which the Father hath put in his own power. ⁸ But ye shall receive power, after that the Holy Ghost is come upon you; and ye shall be witnesses unto me both in Jerusalem, and in all Judaea, and in Samaria, and unto the uttermost part of the earth.' ⁹ And when he had spoken these things, while they beheld, he was taken up; and a cloud received him out of their sight. ¹⁰ And while they looked stedfastly toward heaven as he went up, behold, two men stood by them in white apparel, ¹¹which also said, 'Ye men of Galilee, why stand ye gazing up into heaven? This same Jesus, which is taken up from you into heaven, shall so come in like manner as ye have seen him go into heaven.' ¹²Then returned they unto Jerusalem from the mount called Olivet, which is from Jerusalem a sabbath day's journey. ¹³And when they were come in, they went up into an upper room, where abode both Peter, and James, and John, and Andrew, Philip, and Thomas, Bartholomew, and Matthew, James the son of Alphaeus, and Simon Zelotes, and Judas the brother of James. ¹⁴These all continued with one accord in prayer and supplication, with the women, and Mary the mother of Jesus, and with his brethren.

¹⁵And in those days Peter stood up in the midst of the disciples, and said (the number of names together were about an hundred and twenty), ¹⁶'Men and brethren, this scripture must needs have been fulfilled, which the Holy Ghost by the mouth of David spake before concerning Judas, which was guide to them that took Jesus. ¹⁷For he was numbered with us, and had obtained part of this ministry.' ¹⁸Now this man purchased a field with the reward of iniquity; and falling headlong, he burst asunder in the midst, and all his bowels gushed out. ¹⁹And it was known unto all the dwellers at Jerusalem; insomuch as that field is called in their proper tongue, Aceldama, that is to say, 'The field of blood'. ²⁰'For it is written in the book of Psalms, "Let his habitation be desolate, and let no man dwell therein; and his bishoprick let another take." ²¹Wherefore of these men which have companied with us all the time that the Lord

Jesus went in and out among us, [22] beginning from the baptism of John, unto that same day that he was taken up from us, must one be ordained to be a witness with us of his resurrection.' [23] And they appointed two, Joseph called Barsabas, who was surnamed Justus, and Matthias. [24] And they prayed, and said, 'Thou, Lord, which knowest the hearts of all men, shew whether of these two thou hast chosen, [25] that he may take part of this ministry and apostleship, from which Judas by transgression fell, that he might go to his own place.' [26] And they gave forth their lots; and the lot fell upon Matthias; and he was numbered with the eleven apostles.

2 And when the day of Pentecost was fully come, they were all with one accord in one place. [2] And suddenly there came a sound from heaven as of a rushing mighty wind, and it filled all the house where they were sitting. [3] And there appeared unto them cloven tongues like as of fire, and it sat upon each of them. [4] And they were all filled with the Holy Ghost, and began to speak with other tongues, as the Spirit gave them utterance. [5] And there were dwelling at Jerusalem Jews, devout men, out of every nation under heaven. [6] Now when this was noised abroad, the multitude came together, and were confounded, because that every man heard them speak in his own language. [7] And they were all amazed and marvelled, saying one to another, 'Behold, are not all these which speak Galilæans? [8] And how hear we every man in our own tongue, wherein we were born? [9] Parthians, and Medes, and Elamites, and the dwellers

in Mesopotamia, and in Judaea, and Cappadocia, in Pontus, and Asia, ¹⁰ Phrygia, and Pamphylia, in Egypt, and in the parts of Libya about Cyrene, and strangers of Rome, Jews and proselytes, ¹¹ Cretes and Arabians, we do hear them speak in our tongues the wonderful works of God.' ¹² And they were all amazed, and were in doubt, saying one to another, 'What meaneth this?' ¹³ Others mocking said, 'These men are full of new wine.'

¹⁴ But Peter, standing up with the eleven, lifted up his voice, and said unto them, 'Ye men of Judaea, and all ye that dwell at Jerusalem, be this known unto you, and hearken to my words, ¹⁵ for these are not drunken, as ye suppose, seeing it is but the third hour of the day. ¹⁶ But this is that which was spoken by the prophet Joel: ¹⁷ "And it shall come to pass in the last days," saith God, "I will pour out of my Spirit upon all flesh: and your sons and your daughters shall prophesy, and your young men shall see visions, and your old men shall dream dreams. ¹⁸ And on my servants and on my hand-maidens I will pour out in those days of my Spirit; and they shall prophesy. ¹⁹ And I will shew wonders in heaven above, and signs in the earth beneath; blood, and fire, and vapour of smoke. ²⁰ The sun shall be turned into darkness, and the moon into blood, before that great and notable day of the Lord come. ²¹ And it shall come to pass, that whosoever shall call on the name of the Lord shall be saved." ²² Ye men of Israel, hear these words; Jesus of Nazareth, a man approved of God among you by miracles and wonders and signs, which God did by him in the midst of you, as ye yourselves also know: ²³ him, being delivered by the determinate counsel

and foreknowledge of God, ye have taken, and by wicked hands have crucified and slain, ^{24} whom God hath raised up, having loosed the pains of death, because it was not possible that he should be holden of it. ^{25} For David speaketh concerning him, "I foresaw the Lord always before my face, for he is on my right hand, that I should not be moved: ^{26} therefore did my heart rejoice, and my tongue was glad; moreover also my flesh shall rest in hope, ^{27} because thou wilt not leave my soul in hell, neither wilt thou suffer thine Holy One to see corruption. ^{28} Thou hast made known to me the ways of life; thou shalt make me full of joy with thy countenance."

^{29} Men and brethren, let me freely speak unto you of the patriarch David, that he is both dead and buried, and his sepulchre is with us unto this day. ^{30} Therefore being a prophet, and knowing that God had sworn with an oath to him, that of the fruit of his loins, according to the flesh, he would raise up Christ to sit on his throne; ^{31} he seeing this before spake of the resurrection of Christ, that his soul was not left in hell, neither his flesh did see corruption. ^{32} This Jesus hath God raised up, whereof we all are witnesses. ^{33} Therefore being by the right hand of God exalted, and having received of the Father the promise of the Holy Ghost, he hath shed forth this, which ye now see and hear. ^{34} For David is not ascended into the heavens; but he saith himself, "The Lord said unto my Lord, 'Sit thou on my right hand, ^{35} until I make thy foes thy footstool.'" ^{36} Therefore let all the house of Israel know assuredly, that God hath made that same Jesus, whom ye have crucified, both Lord and Christ.'

^{37} Now when they heard this, they were pricked in their heart, and said unto Peter and to the rest of the apostles, 'Men and brethren, what shall we do?' [38] Then Peter said unto them, 'Repent, and be baptized every one of you in the name of Jesus Christ for the remission of sins, and ye shall receive the gift of the Holy Ghost. [39] For the promise is unto you, and to your children, and to all that are afar off, even as many as the Lord our God shall call.' [40] And with many other words did he testify and exhort, saying, 'Save yourselves from this untoward generation.'

[41] Then they that gladly received his word were baptized: and the same day there were added unto them about three thousand souls. [42] And they continued stedfastly in the apostles' doctrine and fellowship, and in breaking of bread, and in prayers. [43] And fear came upon every soul: and many wonders and signs were done by the apostles. [44] And all that believed were together, and had all things common; [45] and sold their possessions and goods, and parted them to all men, as every man had need. [46] And they, continuing daily with one accord in the temple, and breaking bread from house to house, did eat their meat with gladness and singleness of heart, [47] praising God, and having favour with all the people. And the Lord added to the church daily such as should be saved.

3 Now Peter and John went up together into the temple at the hour of prayer, being the ninth hour. [2] And a certain man lame from his mother's womb was carried, whom they laid daily at the gate of the temple which is called Beautiful, to ask alms of them that entered into the temple, [3] who seeing

Peter and John about to go into the temple asked an alms. ⁴And Peter, fastening his eyes upon him with John, said, 'Look on us.' ⁵And he gave heed unto them, expecting to receive something of them. ⁶Then Peter said, 'Silver and gold have I none; but such as I have give I thee: in the name of Jesus Christ of Nazareth rise up and walk.' ⁷And he took him by the right hand, and lifted him up: and immediately his feet and ankle bones received strength. ⁸And he leaping up stood, and walked, and entered with them into the temple, walking, and leaping, and praising God. ⁹And all the people saw him walking and praising God; ¹⁰and they knew that it was he which sat for alms at the Beautiful gate of the temple; and they were filled with wonder and amazement at that which had happened unto him. ¹¹And as the lame man which was healed held Peter and John, all the people ran together unto them in the porch that is called Solomon's, greatly wondering.

¹²And when Peter saw it, he answered unto the people, 'Ye men of Israel, why marvel ye at this? Or why look ye so earnestly on us, as though by our own power or holiness we had made this man to walk? ¹³The God of Abraham, and of Isaac, and of Jacob, the God of our fathers, hath glorified his Son Jesus; whom ye delivered up, and denied him in the presence of Pilate, when he was determined to let him go. ¹⁴But ye denied the Holy One and the Just, and desired a murderer to be granted unto you; ¹⁵and killed the Prince of life, whom God hath raised from the dead; whereof we are witnesses. ¹⁶And his name through faith in his name hath made this man strong, whom ye see and know: yea, the faith

which is by him hath given him this perfect soundness in the presence of you all. [17]And now, brethren, I wot that through ignorance ye did it, as did also your rulers. [18]But those things, which God before had shewed by the mouth of all his prophets, that Christ should suffer, he hath so fulfilled.

[19]'Repent ye therefore, and be converted, that your sins may be blotted out, when the times of refreshing shall come from the presence of the Lord; [20]and he shall send Jesus Christ, which before was preached unto you, [21]whom the heaven must receive until the times of restitution of all things, which God hath spoken by the mouth of all his holy prophets since the world began. [22]For Moses truly said unto the fathers, "A prophet shall the Lord your God raise up unto you of your brethren, like unto me; him shall ye hear in all things whatsoever he shall say unto you. [23]And it shall come to pass, that every soul, which will not hear that prophet, shall be destroyed from among the people." [24]Yea, and all the prophets from Samuel and those that follow after, as many as have spoken, have likewise foretold of these days. [25]Ye are the children of the prophets, and of the covenant which God made with our fathers, saying unto Abraham, "And in thy seed shall all the kindreds of the earth be blessed." [26]Unto you first God, having raised up his Son Jesus, sent him to bless you, in turning away every one of you from his iniquities.'

4 And as they spake unto the people, the priests, and the captain of the temple, and the Sadducees, came upon them, [2]being grieved that they taught the people, and

preached through Jesus the resurrection from the dead. ³And they laid hands on them, and put them in hold unto the next day, for it was now eventide. ⁴Howbeit many of them which heard the word believed; and the number of the men was about five thousand.

⁵And it came to pass on the morrow, that their rulers, and elders, and scribes, ⁶and Annas the high priest, and Caiaphas, and John, and Alexander, and as many as were of the kindred of the high priest, were gathered together at Jerusalem. ⁷And when they had set them in the midst, they asked, 'By what power, or by what name, have ye done this?' ⁸Then Peter, filled with the Holy Ghost, said unto them, 'Ye rulers of the people, and elders of Israel, ⁹if we this day be examined of the good deed done to the impotent man, by what means he is made whole; ¹⁰be it known unto you all, and to all the people of Israel, that by the name of Jesus Christ of Nazareth, whom ye crucified, whom God raised from the dead, even by him doth this man stand here before you whole. ¹¹This is the stone which was set at nought of you builders, which is become the head of the corner. ¹²Neither is there salvation in any other, for there is none other name under heaven given among men, whereby we must be saved.'

¹³Now when they saw the boldness of Peter and John, and perceived that they were unlearned and ignorant men, they marvelled; and they took knowledge of them, that they had been with Jesus. ¹⁴And beholding the man which was healed standing with them, they could say nothing against it. ¹⁵But when they had commanded them to go aside out of

the council, they conferred among themselves, ¹⁶ saying, 'What shall we do to these men? For that indeed a notable miracle hath been done by them is manifest to all them that dwell in Jerusalem; and we cannot deny it. ¹⁷ But that it spread no further among the people, let us straitly threaten them, that they speak henceforth to no man in this name.' ¹⁸ And they called them, and commanded them not to speak at all nor teach in the name of Jesus. ¹⁹ But Peter and John answered and said unto them, 'Whether it be right in the sight of God to hearken unto you more than unto God, judge ye. ²⁰ For we cannot but speak the things which we have seen and heard.' ²¹ So when they had further threatened them, they let them go, finding nothing how they might punish them, because of the people, for all men glorified God for that which was done. ²² For the man was above forty years old, on whom this miracle of healing was shewed.

²³ And being let go, they went to their own company, and reported all that the chief priests and elders had said unto them. ²⁴ And when they heard that, they lifted up their voice to God with one accord, and said, 'Lord, thou art God, which hast made heaven, and earth, and the sea, and all that in them is, ²⁵ who by the mouth of thy servant David hast said, "Why did the heathen rage, and the people imagine vain things? ²⁶ The kings of the earth stood up, and the rulers were gathered together against the Lord, and against his Christ." ²⁷ For of a truth against thy holy child Jesus, whom thou hast anointed, both Herod, and Pontius Pilate, with the Gentiles, and the people of Israel, were gathered together, ²⁸ for to do whatsoever thy hand and thy counsel determined

before to be done. ²⁹And now, Lord, behold their threatenings; and grant unto thy servants, that with all boldness they may speak thy word, ³⁰by stretching forth thine hand to heal; and that signs and wonders may be done by the name of thy holy child Jesus.'

³¹And when they had prayed, the place was shaken where they were assembled together; and they were all filled with the Holy Ghost, and they spake the word of God with boldness. ³²And the multitude of them that believed were of one heart and of one soul: neither said any of them that ought of the things which he possessed was his own; but they had all things common. ³³And with great power gave the apostles witness of the resurrection of the Lord Jesus, and great grace was upon them all. ³⁴Neither was there any among them that lacked, for as many as were possessors of lands or houses sold them, and brought the prices of the things that were sold, ³⁵and laid them down at the apostles' feet, and distribution was made unto every man according as he had need. ³⁶And Joses, who by the apostles was surnamed Barnabas (which is, being interpreted, 'the son of consolation'), a Levite, and of the country of Cyprus, ³⁷having land, sold it, and brought the money, and laid it at the apostles' feet.

5 But a certain man named Ananias, with Sapphira his wife, sold a possession, ²and kept back part of the price, his wife also being privy to it, and brought a certain part, and laid it at the apostles' feet. ³But Peter said, 'Ananias, why hath Satan filled thine heart to lie to the Holy Ghost,

and to keep back part of the price of the land? ⁴Whiles it remained, was it not thine own? And after it was sold, was it not in thine own power? Why hast thou conceived this thing in thine heart? Thou hast not lied unto men, but unto God.' ⁵And Ananias hearing these words fell down, and gave up the ghost, and great fear came on all them that heard these things. ⁶And the young men arose, wound him up, and carried him out, and buried him. ⁷And it was about the space of three hours after, when his wife, not knowing what was done, came in. ⁸And Peter answered unto her, 'Tell me whether ye sold the land for so much?' And she said, 'Yea, for so much.' ⁹Then Peter said unto her, 'How is it that ye have agreed together to tempt the Spirit of the Lord? Behold, the feet of them which have buried thy husband are at the door, and shall carry thee out.' ¹⁰Then fell she down straightway at his feet, and yielded up the ghost; and the young men came in, and found her dead, and, carrying her forth, buried her by her husband. ¹¹And great fear came upon all the church, and upon as many as heard these things.

¹²And by the hands of the apostles were many signs and wonders wrought among the people (and they were all with one accord in Solomon's porch; ¹³and of the rest durst no man join himself to them; but the people magnified them; ¹⁴and believers were the more added to the Lord, multitudes both of men and women). ¹⁵Insomuch that they brought forth the sick into the streets, and laid them on beds and couches, that at the least the shadow of Peter passing by might overshadow some of them. ¹⁶There came also a multitude out of the cities round about unto Jerusalem, bringing

sick folks, and them which were vexed with unclean spirits; and they were healed every one.

[17] Then the high priest rose up, and all they that were with him (which is the sect of the Sadducees), and were filled with indignation, [18] and laid their hands on the apostles, and put them in the common prison. [19] But the angel of the Lord by night opened the prison doors, and brought them forth, and said, [20] 'Go, stand and speak in the temple to the people all the words of this life.' [21] And when they heard that, they entered into the temple early in the morning, and taught. But the high priest came, and they that were with him, and called the council together, and all the senate of the children of Israel, and sent to the prison to have them brought. [22] But when the officers came, and found them not in the prison, they returned, and told, [23] saying, 'The prison truly found we shut with all safety, and the keepers standing without before the doors; but when we had opened, we found no man within.' [24] Now when the high priest and the captain of the temple and the chief priests heard these things, they doubted of them whereunto this would grow. [25] Then came one and told them, saying, 'Behold, the men whom ye put in prison are standing in the temple, and teaching the people.' [26] Then went the captain with the officers, and brought them without violence, for they feared the people, lest they should have been stoned. [27] And when they had brought them, they set them before the council; and the high priest asked them, [28] saying, 'Did not we straitly command you that ye should not teach in this name? And, behold, ye have filled Jerusalem with your

doctrine, and intend to bring this man's blood upon us.'

²⁹ Then Peter and the other apostles answered and said, 'We ought to obey God rather than men. ³⁰ The God of our fathers raised up Jesus, whom ye slew and hanged on a tree. ³¹ Him hath God exalted with his right hand to be a Prince and a Saviour, for to give repentance to Israel, and forgiveness of sins. ³² And we are his witnesses of these things; and so is also the Holy Ghost, whom God hath given to them that obey him.'

³³ When they heard that, they were cut to the heart, and took counsel to slay them. ³⁴ Then stood there up one in the council, a Pharisee, named Gamaliel, a doctor of the law, had in reputation among all the people, and commanded to put the apostles forth a little space; ³⁵ and said unto them, 'Ye men of Israel, take heed to yourselves what ye intend to do as touching these men. ³⁶ For before these days rose up Theudas, boasting himself to be somebody, to whom a number of men, about four hundred, joined themselves; who was slain; and all, as many as obeyed him, were scattered, and brought to nought. ³⁷ After this man rose up Judas of Galilee in the days of the taxing, and drew away much people after him: he also perished; and all, even as many as obeyed him, were dispersed. ³⁸ And now I say unto you, "Refrain from these men, and let them alone, for if this counsel or this work be of men, it will come to nought; ³⁹ but if it be of God, ye cannot overthrow it; lest haply ye be found even to fight against God."' ⁴⁰ And to him they agreed; and when they had called the apostles, and beaten them, they commanded that they should not speak in the

name of Jesus, and let them go.

⁴¹And they departed from the presence of the council, rejoicing that they were counted worthy to suffer shame for his name. ⁴²And daily in the temple, and in every house, they ceased not to teach and preach Jesus Christ.

6 And in those days, when the number of the disciples was multiplied, there arose a murmuring of the Grecians against the Hebrews, because their widows were neglected in the daily ministration. ²Then the twelve called the multitude of the disciples unto them, and said, 'It is not reason that we should leave the word of God, and serve tables. ³Wherefore, brethren, look ye out among you seven men of honest report, full of the Holy Ghost and wisdom, whom we may appoint over this business. ⁴But we will give ourselves continually to prayer, and to the ministry of the word.'

⁵And the saying pleased the whole multitude; and they chose Stephen, a man full of faith and of the Holy Ghost, and Philip, and Prochorus, and Nicanor, and Timon, and Parmenas, and Nicolas a proselyte of Antioch; ⁶whom they set before the apostles; and when they had prayed, they laid their hands on them. ⁷And the word of God increased; and the number of the disciples multiplied in Jerusalem greatly; and a great company of the priests were obedient to the faith. ⁸And Stephen, full of faith and power, did great wonders and miracles among the people.

⁹Then there arose certain of the synagogue, which is called the synagogue of the Libertines, and Cyrenians, and Alexandrians, and of them of Cilicia and of Asia, disputing with

Stephen. [10] And they were not able to resist the wisdom and the spirit by which he spake. [11] Then they suborned men, which said, 'We have heard him speak blasphemous words against Moses, and against God.' [12] And they stirred up the people, and the elders, and the scribes, and came upon him, and caught him, and brought him to the council, [13] and set up false witnesses, which said, 'This man ceaseth not to speak blasphemous words against this holy place, and the law, [14] for we have heard him say that this Jesus of Nazareth shall destroy this place, and shall change the customs which Moses delivered us.' [15] And all that sat in the council, looking stedfastly on him, saw his face as it had been the face of an angel.

7 Then said the high priest, 'Are these things so?' [2] And he said, 'Men, brethren, and fathers, hearken: the God of glory appeared unto our father Abraham, when he was in Mesopotamia, before he dwelt in Charran, [3] and said unto him, "Get thee out of thy country, and from thy kindred, and come into the land which I shall shew thee." [4] Then came he out of the land of the Chaldaeans, and dwelt in Charran; and from thence, when his father was dead, he removed him into this land, wherein ye now dwell. [5] And he gave him none inheritance in it, no, not so much as to set his foot on: yet he promised that he would give it to him for a possession, and to his seed after him, when as yet he had no child. [6] And God spake on this wise, "That his seed should sojourn in a strange land; and that they should bring them into bondage, and entreat them evil four hundred years. [7] And the nation to

whom they shall be in bondage will I judge," said God; "and after that shall they come forth, and serve me in this place." [8]And he gave him the covenant of circumcision: and so Abraham begat Isaac, and circumcised him the eighth day; and Isaac begat Jacob; and Jacob begat the twelve patriarchs. [9]And the patriarchs, moved with envy, sold Joseph into Egypt; but God was with him, [10]and delivered him out of all his afflictions, and gave him favour and wisdom in the sight of Pharaoh king of Egypt; and he made him governor over Egypt and all his house. [11]Now there came a dearth over all the land of Egypt and Chanaan, and great affliction: and our fathers found no sustenance. [12]But when Jacob heard that there was corn in Egypt, he sent out our fathers first. [13]And at the second time Joseph was made known to his brethren; and Joseph's kindred was made known unto Pharaoh. [14]Then sent Joseph, and called his father Jacob to him, and all his kindred, threescore and fifteen souls. [15]So Jacob went down into Egypt, and died, he, and our fathers, [16]and were carried over into Sychem, and laid in the sepulchre that Abraham bought for a sum of money of the sons of Emmor the father of Sychem. [17]But when the time of the promise drew nigh, which God had sworn to Abraham, the people grew and multiplied in Egypt, [18]till another king arose, which knew not Joseph. [19]The same dealt subtilly with our kindred, and evil entreated our fathers, so that they cast out their young children, to the end they might not live. [20]In which time Moses was born, and was exceeding fair, and nourished up in his father's house three months; [21]and when he was cast out, Pharaoh's daughter took him up, and nourished him for her own son. ²²And Moses was learned in all the wisdom of the Egyptians, and was mighty in words and in deeds. ²³And when he was full forty years old, it came into his heart to visit his brethren the children of Israel. ²⁴And seeing one of them suffer wrong, he defended him, and avenged him that was oppressed, and smote the Egyptian, ²⁵for he supposed his brethren would have understood how that God by his hand would deliver them: but they understood not. ²⁶And the next day he shewed himself unto them as they strove, and would have set them at one again, saying, "Sirs, ye are brethren; why do ye wrong one to another?" ²⁷But he that did his neighbour wrong thrust him away, saying, "Who made thee a ruler and a judge over us? ²⁸Wilt thou kill me, as thou diddest the Egyptian yesterday?" ²⁹Then fled Moses at this saying, and was a stranger in the land of Madian, where he begat two sons. ³⁰And when forty years were expired, there appeared to him in the wilderness of mount Sina an angel of the Lord in a flame of fire in a bush. ³¹When Moses saw it, he wondered at the sight; and as he drew near to behold it, the voice of the Lord came unto him, ³²saying, "I am the God of thy fathers, the God of Abraham, and the God of Isaac, and the God of Jacob." Then Moses trembled, and durst not behold. ³³Then said the Lord to him, "Put off thy shoes from thy feet, for the place where thou standest is holy ground. ³⁴I have seen, I have seen the affliction of my people which is in Egypt, and I have heard their groaning, and am come down to deliver them. And now come, I will send thee into Egypt." ³⁵This Moses whom they refused, saying, "Who made thee a ruler and a judge?", the same did God send to be a ruler and a deliverer by the hand of the angel which appeared to him in the bush. ³⁶ He brought them out, after that he had shewed wonders and signs in the land of Egypt, and in the Red Sea, and in the wilderness forty years.

³⁷ 'This is that Moses, which said unto the children of Israel, "A prophet shall the Lord your God raise up unto you of your brethren, like unto me; him shall ye hear." ³⁸ This is he, that was in the church in the wilderness with the angel which spake to him in the mount Sina, and with our fathers, who received the lively oracles to give unto us, ³⁹ to whom our fathers would not obey, but thrust him from them, and in their hearts turned back again into Egypt, ⁴⁰ saying unto Aaron, "Make us gods to go before us, for as for this Moses, which brought us out of the land of Egypt, we wot not what is become of him." ⁴¹ And they made a calf in those days, and offered sacrifice unto the idol, and rejoiced in the works of their own hands. ⁴² Then God turned, and gave them up to worship the host of heaven; as it is written in the book of the prophets, "O ye house of Israel, have ye offered to me slain beasts and sacrifices by the space of forty years in the wilderness? ⁴³ Yea, ye took up the tabernacle of Moloch, and the star of your god Remphan, figures which ye made to worship them, and I will carry you away beyond Babylon." ⁴⁴ Our fathers had the tabernacle of witness in the wilderness, as he had appointed, speaking unto Moses, that he should make it according to the fashion that he had seen. ⁴⁵ Which also our fathers that came after brought in with Jesus into the possession of the Gentiles, whom God drave

out before the face of our fathers, unto the days of David, ⁴⁶ who found favour before God, and desired to find a tabernacle for the God of Jacob. ⁴⁷ But Solomon built him an house. ⁴⁸ Howbeit the most High dwelleth not in temples made with hands; as saith the prophet, ⁴⁹"Heaven is my throne, and earth is my footstool: what house will ye build me? saith the Lord: or what is the place of my rest? ⁵⁰ Hath not my hand made all these things?"

⁵¹ 'Ye stiffnecked and uncircumcised in heart and ears, ye do always resist the Holy Ghost: as your fathers did, so do ye. ⁵² Which of the prophets have not your fathers persecuted? And they have slain them which shewed before of the coming of the Just One; of whom ye have been now the betrayers and murderers; ⁵³ who have received the law by the disposition of angels, and have not kept it.'

⁵⁴ When they heard these things, they were cut to the heart, and they gnashed on him with their teeth. ⁵⁵ But he, being full of the Holy Ghost, looked up stedfastly into heaven, and saw the glory of God, and Jesus standing on the right hand of God, ⁵⁶ and said, 'Behold, I see the heavens opened, and the Son of man standing on the right hand of God.' ⁵⁷ Then they cried out with a loud voice, and stopped their ears, and ran upon him with one accord, ⁵⁸ and cast him out of the city, and stoned him: and the witnesses laid down their clothes at a young man's feet, whose name was Saul. ⁵⁹ And they stoned Stephen, calling upon God, and saying, 'Lord Jesus, receive my spirit.' ⁶⁰ And he kneeled down, and cried with a loud voice, 'Lord, lay not this sin to their charge.' And when he had said this, he fell asleep.

8 And Saul was consenting unto his death. And at that time there was a great persecution against the church which was at Jerusalem; and they were all scattered abroad throughout the regions of Judaea and Samaria, except the apostles. ²And devout men carried Stephen to his burial, and made great lamentation over him. ³As for Saul, he made havock of the church, entering into every house, and haling men and women committed them to prison.

⁴Therefore they that were scattered abroad went every where preaching the word. ⁵Then Philip went down to the city of Samaria, and preached Christ unto them. ⁶And the people with one accord gave heed unto those things which Philip spake, hearing and seeing the miracles which he did. ⁷For unclean spirits, crying with loud voice, came out of many that were possessed with them: and many taken with palsies, and that were lame, were healed. ⁸And there was great joy in that city.

⁹But there was a certain man, called Simon, which before-time in the same city used sorcery, and bewitched the people of Samaria, giving out that himself was some great one, ¹⁰to whom they all gave heed, from the least to the greatest, say-ing, 'This man is the great power of God.' ¹¹And to him they had regard, because that of long time he had bewitched them with sorceries. ¹²But when they believed Philip preach-ing the things concerning the kingdom of God, and the name of Jesus Christ, they were baptized, both men and women. ¹³Then Simon himself believed also: and when he was baptized, he continued with Philip, and wondered, beholding the miracles and signs which were done.

¹⁴ Now when the apostles which were at Jerusalem heard that Samaria had received the word of God, they sent unto them Peter and John, ¹⁵ who, when they were come down, prayed for them, that they might receive the Holy Ghost ¹⁶(for as yet he was fallen upon none of them: only they were baptized in the name of the Lord Jesus). ¹⁷ Then laid they their hands on them, and they received the Holy Ghost. ¹⁸And when Simon saw that through laying on of the apostles' hands the Holy Ghost was given, he offered them money, ¹⁹ saying, 'Give me also this power, that on whomsoever I lay hands, he may receive the Holy Ghost.' ²⁰ But Peter said unto him, 'Thy money perish with thee, because thou hast thought that the gift of God may be purchased with money. ²¹ Thou hast neither part nor lot in this matter, for thy heart is not right in the sight of God. ²² Repent therefore of this thy wickedness, and pray God, if perhaps the thought of thine heart may be forgiven thee. ²³ For I perceive that thou art in the gall of bitterness, and in the bond of iniquity.' ²⁴ Then answered Simon, and said, 'Pray ye to the Lord for me, that none of these things which ye have spoken come upon me.'

²⁵And they, when they had testified and preached the word of the Lord, returned to Jerusalem, and preached the gospel in many villages of the Samaritans.

²⁶And the angel of the Lord spake unto Philip, saying, 'Arise, and go toward the south unto the way that goeth down from Jerusalem unto Gaza, which is desert.' ²⁷And he arose and went: and, behold, a man of Ethiopia, an eunuch of great authority under Candace queen of the Ethiopians,

who had the charge of all her treasure, and had come to Jerusalem for to worship, ²⁸ was returning, and sitting in his chariot read Esaias the prophet. ²⁹ Then the Spirit said unto Philip, 'Go near, and join thyself to this chariot.' ³⁰And Philip ran thither to him, and heard him read the prophet Esaias, and said, 'Understandest thou what thou readest?' ³¹And he said, 'How can I, except some man should guide me?' And he desired Philip that he would come up and sit with him. ³² The place of the scripture which he read was this, 'He was led as a sheep to the slaughter; and like a lamb dumb before his shearer, so opened he not his mouth. ³³ In his humiliation his judgment was taken away: and who shall declare his generation? For his life is taken from the earth.' ³⁴And the eunuch answered Philip, and said, 'I pray thee, of whom speaketh the prophet this? Of himself, or of some other man?' ³⁵ Then Philip opened his mouth, and began at the same scripture, and preached unto him Jesus. ³⁶And as they went on their way, they came unto a certain water: and the eunuch said, 'See, here is water; what doth hinder me to be baptized?' ³⁷And Philip said, 'If thou believest with all thine heart, thou mayest.' And he answered and said, 'I believe that Jesus Christ is the Son of God.' ³⁸And he commanded the chariot to stand still: and they went down both into the water, both Philip and the eunuch; and he baptized him. ³⁹And when they were come up out of the water, the Spirit of the Lord caught away Philip, that the eunuch saw him no more: and he went on his way rejoicing. ⁴⁰ But Philip was found at Azotus: and passing through he preached in all the cities, till he came to Caesarea.

9 And Saul, yet breathing out threatenings and slaughter against the disciples of the Lord, went unto the high priest, ²and desired of him letters to Damascus to the synagogues, that if he found any of this way, whether they were men or women, he might bring them bound unto Jerusalem. ³And as he journeyed, he came near Damascus; and suddenly there shined round about him a light from heaven; ⁴and he fell to the earth, and heard a voice saying unto him, 'Saul, Saul, why persecutest thou me?' ⁵And he said, 'Who art thou, Lord?' And the Lord said, 'I am Jesus whom thou persecutest: it is hard for thee to kick against the pricks.' ⁶And he trembling and astonished said, 'Lord, what wilt thou have me to do?' And the Lord said unto him, 'Arise, and go into the city, and it shall be told thee what thou must do.' ⁷And the men which journeyed with him stood speechless, hearing a voice, but seeing no man. ⁸And Saul arose from the earth; and when his eyes were opened, he saw no man; but they led him by the hand, and brought him into Damascus. ⁹And he was three days without sight, and neither did eat nor drink.

¹⁰And there was a certain disciple at Damascus, named Ananias; and to him said the Lord in a vision, 'Ananias'. And he said, 'Behold, I am here, Lord.' ¹¹And the Lord said unto him, 'Arise, and go into the street which is called Straight, and enquire in the house of Judas for one called Saul, of Tarsus, for, behold, he prayeth, ¹²and hath seen in a vision a man named Ananias coming in, and putting his hand on him, that he might receive his sight.' ¹³Then Ananias answered, 'Lord, I have heard by many of this man, how

much evil he hath done to thy saints at Jerusalem, [14] and here he hath authority from the chief priests to bind all that call on thy name.' [15] But the Lord said unto him, 'Go thy way, for he is a chosen vessel unto me, to bear my name before the Gentiles, and kings, and the children of Israel, [16] for I will shew him how great things he must suffer for my name's sake.' [17] And Ananias went his way, and entered into the house; and putting his hands on him said, 'Brother Saul, the Lord, even Jesus, that appeared unto thee in the way as thou camest, hath sent me, that thou mightest receive thy sight, and be filled with the Holy Ghost.' [18] And immediately there fell from his eyes as it had been scales; and he received sight forthwith, and arose, and was baptized. [19] And when he had received meat, he was strengthened. Then was Saul certain days with the disciples which were at Damascus. [20] And straightway he preached Christ in the synagogues, that he is the Son of God. [21] But all that heard him were amazed, and said, 'Is not this he that destroyed them which called on this name in Jerusalem, and came hither for that intent, that he might bring them bound unto the chief priests?' [22] But Saul increased the more in strength, and confounded the Jews which dwelt at Damascus, proving that this is very Christ.

[23] And after that many days were fulfilled, the Jews took counsel to kill him, [24] but their laying await was known of Saul. And they watched the gates day and night to kill him. [25] Then the disciples took him by night, and let him down by the wall in a basket. [26] And when Saul was come to Jerusalem, he assayed to join himself to the disciples, but they were all afraid of him, and believed not that he was a

disciple. ²⁷ But Barnabas took him, and brought him to the apostles, and declared unto them how he had seen the Lord in the way, and that he had spoken to him, and how he had preached boldly at Damascus in the name of Jesus. ²⁸And he was with them coming in and going out at Jerusalem. ²⁹And he spake boldly in the name of the Lord Jesus, and disputed against the Grecians, but they went about to slay him, ³⁰ which when the brethren knew, they brought him down to Caesarea, and sent him forth to Tarsus. ³¹Then had the churches rest throughout all Judaea and Galilee and Samaria, and were edified; and walking in the fear of the Lord, and in the comfort of the Holy Ghost, were multiplied.

³²And it came to pass, as Peter passed throughout all quarters, he came down also to the saints which dwelt at Lydda. ³³And there he found a certain man named Aeneas, which had kept his bed eight years, and was sick of the palsy. ³⁴And Peter said unto him, 'Aeneas, Jesus Christ maketh thee whole: arise, and make thy bed.' And he arose immediately. ³⁵And all that dwelt at Lydda and Saron saw him, and turned to the Lord.

³⁶ Now there was at Joppa a certain disciple named Tabitha, which by interpretation is called Dorcas: this woman was full of good works and almsdeeds which she did. ³⁷And it came to pass in those days, that she was sick, and died, whom when they had washed, they laid her in an upper chamber. ³⁸And forasmuch as Lydda was nigh to Joppa, and the disciples had heard that Peter was there, they sent unto him two men, desiring him that he would not delay to come to them. ³⁹ Then Peter arose and went with

them. When he was come, they brought him into the upper chamber: and all the widows stood by him weeping, and shewing the coats and garments which Dorcas made, while she was with them. ⁴⁰But Peter put them all forth, and kneeled down, and prayed; and turning him to the body said, 'Tabitha, arise.' And she opened her eyes, and when she saw Peter, she sat up. ⁴¹And he gave her his hand, and lifted her up, and when he had called the saints and widows, presented her alive. ⁴²And it was known throughout all Joppa; and many believed in the Lord. ⁴³And it came to pass, that he tarried many days in Joppa with one Simon a tanner.

10 There was a certain man in Caesarea called Cornelius, a centurion of the band called the Italian band, ²a devout man, and one that feared God with all his house, which gave much alms to the people, and prayed to God alway. ³He saw in a vision evidently about the ninth hour of the day an angel of God coming in to him, and saying unto him, 'Cornelius'. ⁴And when he looked on him, he was afraid, and said, 'What is it, Lord?' And he said unto him, 'Thy prayers and thine alms are come up for a memorial before God. ⁵And now send men to Joppa, and call for one Simon, whose surname is Peter: ⁶he lodgeth with one Simon a tanner, whose house is by the sea side: he shall tell thee what thou oughtest to do.' ⁷And when the angel which spake unto Cornelius was departed, he called two of his household servants, and a devout soldier of them that waited on him continually; ⁸and when he had declared all these things unto them, he sent them to Joppa.

⁹On the morrow, as they went on their journey, and drew nigh unto the city, Peter went up upon the housetop to pray about the sixth hour. ¹⁰And he became very hungry, and would have eaten, but while they made ready, he fell into a trance, ¹¹and saw heaven opened, and a certain vessel descending unto him, as it had been a great sheet knit at the four corners, and let down to the earth, ¹²wherein were all manner of four-footed beasts of the earth, and wild beasts, and creeping things, and fowls of the air. ¹³And there came a voice to him, 'Rise, Peter; kill, and eat.' ¹⁴But Peter said, 'Not so, Lord; for I have never eaten any thing that is common or unclean.' ¹⁵And the voice spake unto him again the second time, 'What God hath cleansed, that call not thou common.' ¹⁶This was done thrice, and the vessel was received up again into heaven. ¹⁷Now while Peter doubted in himself what this vision which he had seen should mean, behold, the men which were sent from Cornelius had made enquiry for Simon's house, and stood before the gate, ¹⁸and called, and asked whether Simon, which was surnamed Peter, were lodged there.

¹⁹While Peter thought on the vision, the Spirit said unto him, 'Behold, three men seek thee. ²⁰Arise therefore, and get thee down, and go with them, doubting nothing, for I have sent them.' ²¹Then Peter went down to the men which were sent unto him from Cornelius; and said, 'Behold, I am he whom ye seek: what is the cause wherefore ye are come?' ²²And they said, 'Cornelius the centurion, a just man, and one that feareth God, and of good report among all the nation of the Jews, was warned from God by an holy angel

to send for thee into his house, and to hear words of thee.' [23] Then called he them in, and lodged them. And on the morrow Peter went away with them, and certain brethren from Joppa accompanied him. [24] And the morrow after they entered into Caesarea. And Cornelius waited for them, and had called together his kinsmen and near friends. [25] And as Peter was coming in, Cornelius met him, and fell down at his feet, and worshipped him. [26] But Peter took him up, saying, 'Stand up; I myself also am a man.' [27] And as he talked with him, he went in, and found many that were come together. [28] And he said unto them, 'Ye know how that it is an unlawful thing for a man that is a Jew to keep company, or come unto one of another nation; but God hath shewed me that I should not call any man common or unclean. [29] Therefore came I unto you without gainsaying, as soon as I was sent for: I ask therefore for what intent ye have sent for me?' [30] And Cornelius said, 'Four days ago I was fasting until this hour; and at the ninth hour I prayed in my house, and, behold, a man stood before me in bright clothing, [31] and said, "Cornelius, thy prayer is heard, and thine alms are had in remembrance in the sight of God. [32] Send therefore to Joppa, and call hither Simon, whose surname is Peter; he is lodged in the house of one Simon a tanner by the sea side: who, when he cometh, shall speak unto thee." [33] Immediately therefore I sent to thee; and thou hast well done that thou art come. Now therefore are we all here present before God, to hear all things that are commanded thee of God.'

[34] Then Peter opened his mouth, and said, 'Of a truth I perceive that God is no respecter of persons, [35] but in every

nation he that feareth him, and worketh righteousness, is accepted with him. ³⁶ The word which God sent unto the children of Israel, preaching peace by Jesus Christ (he is Lord of all). ³⁷ That word, I say, ye know, which was published throughout all Judaea, and began from Galilee, after the baptism which John preached; ³⁸ how God anointed Jesus of Nazareth with the Holy Ghost and with power; who went about doing good, and healing all that were oppressed of the devil; for God was with him. ³⁹ And we are witnesses of all things which he did both in the land of the Jews, and in Jerusalem; whom they slew and hanged on a tree: ⁴⁰ Him God raised up the third day, and shewed him openly; ⁴¹ not to all the people, but unto witnesses chosen before of God, even to us, who did eat and drink with him after he rose from the dead. ⁴² And he commanded us to preach unto the people, and to testify that it is he which was ordained of God to be the Judge of quick and dead. ⁴³ To him give all the prophets witness, that through his name whosoever believeth in him shall receive remission of sins.'

⁴⁴ While Peter yet spake these words, the Holy Ghost fell on all them which heard the word. ⁴⁵ And they of the circumcision which believed were astonished, as many as came with Peter, because that on the Gentiles also was poured out the gift of the Holy Ghost. ⁴⁶ For they heard them speak with tongues, and magnify God. Then answered Peter, ⁴⁷ 'Can any man forbid water, that these should not be baptized, which have received the Holy Ghost as well as we?' ⁴⁸ And he commanded them to be baptized in the name of the Lord. Then prayed they him to tarry certain days.

11 And the apostles and brethren that were in Judaea heard that the Gentiles had also received the word of God. ²And when Peter was come up to Jerusalem, they that were of the circumcision contended with him, ³saying, 'Thou wentest in to men uncircumcised, and didst eat with them.' ⁴But Peter rehearsed the matter from the beginning, and expounded it by order unto them, saying, ⁵'I was in the city of Joppa praying: and in a trance I saw a vision, a certain vessel descend, as it had been a great sheet, let down from heaven by four corners; and it came even to me; ⁶upon the which when I had fastened mine eyes, I considered, and saw four-footed beasts of the earth, and wild beasts, and creeping things, and fowls of the air. ⁷And I heard a voice saying unto me, "Arise, Peter; slay and eat." ⁸But I said, "Not so, Lord: for nothing common or unclean hath at any time entered into my mouth." ⁹But the voice answered me again from heaven, "What God hath cleansed, that call not thou common." ¹⁰And this was done three times: and all were drawn up again into heaven. ¹¹And, behold, immediately there were three men already come unto the house where I was, sent from Caesarea unto me. ¹²And the Spirit bade me go with them, nothing doubting. Moreover these six brethren accompanied me, and we entered into the man's house: ¹³and he shewed us how he had seen an angel in his house, which stood and said unto him, "Send men to Joppa, and call for Simon, whose surname is Peter; ¹⁴who shall tell thee words, whereby thou and all thy house shall be saved." ¹⁵And as I began to speak, the Holy Ghost fell on them, as on us at the beginning. ¹⁶Then remembered I the word of the

Lord, how that he said, "John indeed baptized with water; but ye shall be baptized with the Holy Ghost." [17] Forasmuch then as God gave them the like gift as he did unto us, who believed on the Lord Jesus Christ; what was I, that I could withstand God?' [18] When they heard these things, they held their peace, and glorified God, saying, 'Then hath God also to the Gentiles granted repentance unto life.'

[19] Now they which were scattered abroad upon the persecution that arose about Stephen travelled as far as Phenice, and Cyprus, and Antioch, preaching the word to none but unto the Jews only. [20] And some of them were men of Cyprus and Cyrene, which, when they were come to Antioch, spake unto the Grecians, preaching the Lord Jesus. [21] And the hand of the Lord was with them: and a great number believed, and turned unto the Lord.

[22] Then tidings of these things came unto the ears of the church which was in Jerusalem: and they sent forth Barnabas, that he should go as far as Antioch. [23] Who, when he came, and had seen the grace of God, was glad, and exhorted them all, that with purpose of heart they would cleave unto the Lord. [24] For he was a good man, and full of the Holy Ghost and of faith: and much people was added unto the Lord. [25] Then departed Barnabas to Tarsus, for to seek Saul; [26] and when he had found him, he brought him unto Antioch. And it came to pass, that a whole year they assembled themselves with the church, and taught much people. And the disciples were called Christians first in Antioch.

[27] And in these days came prophets from Jerusalem unto

Antioch. ²⁸And there stood up one of them named Agabus, and signified by the Spirit that there should be great dearth throughout all the world; which came to pass in the days of Claudius Caesar. ²⁹Then the disciples, every man according to his ability, determined to send relief unto the brethren which dwelt in Judaea; ³⁰which also they did, and sent it to the elders by the hands of Barnabas and Saul.

12 Now about that time Herod the king stretched forth his hands to vex certain of the church. ²And he killed James the brother of John with the sword. ³And because he saw it pleased the Jews, he proceeded further to take Peter also. (Then were the days of unleavened bread.) ⁴And when he had apprehended him, he put him in prison, and delivered him to four quaternions of soldiers to keep him; intending after Easter to bring him forth to the people. ⁵Peter therefore was kept in prison, but prayer was made without ceasing of the church unto God for him. ⁶And when Herod would have brought him forth, the same night Peter was sleeping between two soldiers, bound with two chains; and the keepers before the door kept the prison. ⁷And, behold, the angel of the Lord came upon him, and a light shined in the prison; and he smote Peter on the side, and raised him up, saying, 'Arise up quickly.' And his chains fell off from his hands. ⁸And the angel said unto him, 'Gird thyself, and bind on thy sandals.' And so he did. And he saith unto him, 'Cast thy garment about thee, and follow me.' ⁹And he went out, and followed him; and wist not that it was true which was done by the angel; but thought he saw a vision. ¹⁰When they were past the first and the second ward, they came unto the iron gate that leadeth unto the city; which opened to them of his own accord: and they went out, and passed on through one street; and forthwith the angel departed from him. ¹¹And when Peter was come to himself, he said, 'Now I know of a surety, that the Lord hath sent his angel, and hath delivered me out of the hand of Herod, and from all the expectation of the people of the Jews.' ¹²And when he had considered the thing, he came to the house of Mary the mother of John, whose surname was Mark; where many were gathered together praying. ¹³And as Peter knocked at the door of the gate, a damsel came to hearken, named Rhoda. ¹⁴And when she knew Peter's voice, she opened not the gate for gladness, but ran in, and told how Peter stood before the gate. ¹⁵And they said unto her, 'Thou art mad.' But she constantly affirmed that it was even so. Then said they, 'It is his angel.' ¹⁶ But Peter continued knocking: and when they had opened the door, and saw him, they were astonished. ¹⁷ But he, beckoning unto them with the hand to hold their peace, declared unto them how the Lord had brought him out of the prison. And he said, 'Go shew these things unto James, and to the brethren.' And he departed, and went into another place. ¹⁸ Now as soon as it was day, there was no small stir among the soldiers, what was become of Peter. ¹⁹And when Herod had sought for him, and found him not, he examined the keepers, and commanded that they should be put to death. And he went down from Judaea to Caesarea, and there abode.

²⁰And Herod was highly displeased with them of Tyre and Sidon; but they came with one accord to him, and, having

made Blastus the king's chamberlain their friend, desired peace; because their country was nourished by the king's country. ²¹And upon a set day Herod, arrayed in royal apparel, sat upon his throne, and made an oration unto them. ²²And the people gave a shout, saying, 'It is the voice of a god, and not of a man.' ²³And immediately the angel of the Lord smote him, because he gave not God the glory; and he was eaten of worms, and gave up the ghost.

²⁴But the word of God grew and multiplied. ²⁵And Barnabas and Saul returned from Jerusalem, when they had fulfilled their ministry, and took with them John, whose surname was Mark.

13 Now there were in the church that was at Antioch certain prophets and teachers; as Barnabas, and Simeon that was called Niger, and Lucius of Cyrene, and Manaen, which had been brought up with Herod the tetrarch, and Saul. ²As they ministered to the Lord, and fasted, the Holy Ghost said, 'Separate me Barnabas and Saul for the work whereunto I have called them.' ³And when they had fasted and prayed, and laid their hands on them, they sent them away.

⁴So they, being sent forth by the Holy Ghost, departed unto Seleucia; and from thence they sailed to Cyprus. ⁵And when they were at Salamis, they preached the word of God in the synagogues of the Jews; and they had also John to their minister. ⁶And when they had gone through the isle unto Paphos, they found a certain sorcerer, a false prophet, a Jew, whose name was Bar-jesus; ⁷which was with the

deputy of the country, Sergius Paulus, a prudent man; who called for Barnabas and Saul, and desired to hear the word of God. ⁸ But Elymas the sorcerer (for so is his name by interpretation) withstood them, seeking to turn away the deputy from the faith. ⁹ Then Saul (who also is called Paul), filled with the Holy Ghost, set his eyes on him, ¹⁰and said, 'O full of all subtilty and all mischief, thou child of the devil, thou enemy of all righteousness, wilt thou not cease to pervert the right ways of the Lord? ¹¹And now, behold, the hand of the Lord is upon thee, and thou shalt be blind, not seeing the sun for a season.' And immediately there fell on him a mist and a darkness; and he went about seeking some to lead him by the hand. ¹²Then the deputy, when he saw what was done, believed, being astonished at the doctrine of the Lord. ¹³Now when Paul and his company loosed from Paphos, they came to Perga in Pamphylia; and John departing from them returned to Jerusalem.

¹⁴But when they departed from Perga, they came to Antioch in Pisidia, and went into the synagogue on the sabbath day, and sat down. ¹⁵And after the reading of the law and the prophets the rulers of the synagogue sent unto them, saying, 'Ye men and brethren, if ye have any word of exhortation for the people, say on.' ¹⁶Then Paul stood up, and beckoning with his hand said, 'Men of Israel, and ye that fear God, give audience. ¹⁷The God of this people of Israel chose our fathers, and exalted the people when they dwelt as strangers in the land of Egypt, and with an high arm brought he them out of it. ¹⁸And about the time of forty years suffered he their manners in the wilderness. ¹⁹And when he had destroyed

seven nations in the land of Chanaan, he divided their land to them by lot. ²⁰And after that he gave unto them judges about the space of four hundred and fifty years, until Samuel the prophet. ²¹And afterward, they desired a king: and God gave unto them Saul the son of Cis, a man of the tribe of Benjamin, by the space of forty years. ²²And when he had removed him, he raised up unto them David to be their king; to whom also he gave testimony, and said, "I have found David the son of Jesse, a man after mine own heart, which shall fulfil all my will." ²³Of this man's seed hath God according to his promise raised unto Israel a Saviour, Jesus; ²⁴when John had first preached before his coming the baptism of repentance to all the people of Israel. ²⁵And as John fulfilled his course, he said, "Whom think ye that I am? I am not he. But, behold, there cometh one after me, whose shoes of his feet I am not worthy to loose." ²⁶Men and brethren, children of the stock of Abraham, and whosoever among you feareth God, to you is the word of this salvation sent. ²⁷For they that dwell at Jerusalem, and their rulers, because they knew him not, nor yet the voices of the prophets which are read every sabbath day, they have fulfilled them in condemning him. ²⁸And though they found no cause of death in him, yet desired they Pilate that he should be slain. ²⁹And when they had fulfilled all that was written of him, they took him down from the tree, and laid him in a sepulchre. ³⁰But God raised him from the dead; ³¹and he was seen many days of them which came up with him from Galilee to Jerusalem, who are his witnesses unto the people. ³²And we declare unto you glad tidings, how that the promise which was made unto the fathers, ³³ God hath fulfilled the same unto us their children, in that he hath raised up Jesus again; as it is also written in the second psalm, "Thou art my Son, this day have I begotten thee." ³⁴ And as concerning that he raised him up from the dead, now no more to return to corruption, he said on this wise, "I will give you the sure mercies of David." ³⁵ Wherefore he saith also in another psalm, "Thou shalt not suffer thine Holy One to see corruption." ³⁶ For David, after he had served his own generation by the will of God, fell on sleep, and was laid unto his fathers, and saw corruption, ³⁷ but he, whom God raised again, saw no corruption.

³⁸ 'Be it known unto you therefore, men and brethren, that through this man is preached unto you the forgiveness of sins; ³⁹ and by him all that believe are justified from all things, from which ye could not be justified by the law of Moses. ⁴⁰ Beware therefore, lest that come upon you, which is spoken of in the prophets: ⁴¹ "Behold, ye despisers, and wonder, and perish; for I work a work in your days, a work which ye shall in no wise believe, though a man declare it unto you."' ⁴² And when the Jews were gone out of the synagogue, the Gentiles besought that these words might be preached to them the next sabbath. ⁴³ Now when the congregation was broken up, many of the Jews and religious proselytes followed Paul and Barnabas; who, speaking to them, persuaded them to continue in the grace of God.

⁴⁴ And the next sabbath day came almost the whole city together to hear the word of God. ⁴⁵ But when the Jews saw the multitudes, they were filled with envy, and spake

against those things which were spoken by Paul, contradicting and blaspheming. ⁴⁶ Then Paul and Barnabas waxed bold, and said, 'It was necessary that the word of God should first have been spoken to you; but seeing ye put it from you, and judge yourselves unworthy of everlasting life, lo, we turn to the Gentiles.' ⁴⁷ For so hath the Lord commanded us, saying, 'I have set thee to be a light of the Gentiles, that thou shouldest be for salvation unto the ends of the earth.' ⁴⁸ And when the Gentiles heard this, they were glad, and glorified the word of the Lord: and as many as were ordained to eternal life believed. ⁴⁹ And the word of the Lord was published throughout all the region. ⁵⁰ But the Jews stirred up the devout and honourable women, and the chief men of the city, and raised persecution against Paul and Barnabas, and expelled them out of their coasts. ⁵¹ But they shook off the dust of their feet against them, and came unto Iconium. ⁵² And the disciples were filled with joy, and with the Holy Ghost.

14 And it came to pass in Iconium, that they went both together into the synagogue of the Jews, and so spake, that a great multitude both of the Jews and also of the Greeks believed. ² But the unbelieving Jews stirred up the Gentiles, and made their minds evil affected against the brethren. ³ Long time therefore abode they speaking boldly in the Lord, which gave testimony unto the word of his grace, and granted signs and wonders to be done by their hands. ⁴ But the multitude of the city was divided: and part held with the Jews, and part with the apostles. ⁵ And when

there was an assault made both of the Gentiles, and also of the Jews with their rulers, to use them despitefully, and to stone them, ⁶ they were ware of it, and fled unto Lystra and Derbe, cities of Lycaonia, and unto the region that lieth round about; ⁷and there they preached the gospel.

⁸And there sat a certain man at Lystra, impotent in his feet, being a cripple from his mother's womb, who never had walked: ⁹ the same heard Paul speak, who stedfastly beholding him, and perceiving that he had faith to be healed, ¹⁰said with a loud voice, 'Stand upright on thy feet.' And he leaped and walked. ¹¹And when the people saw what Paul had done, they lifted up their voices, saying in the speech of Lycaonia, 'The gods are come down to us in the likeness of men.' ¹²And they called Barnabas, Jupiter; and Paul, Mercurius, because he was the chief speaker. ¹³ Then the priest of Jupiter, which was before their city, brought oxen and garlands unto the gates, and would have done sacrifice with the people. ¹⁴Which when the apostles, Barnabas and Paul, heard of, they rent their clothes, and ran in among the people, crying out, ¹⁵ and saying, 'Sirs, why do ye these things? We also are men of like passions with you, and preach unto you that ye should turn from these vanities unto the living God, which made heaven, and earth, and the sea, and all things that are therein, ¹⁶ who in times past suffered all nations to walk in their own ways. ¹⁷ Nevertheless he left not himself without witness, in that he did good, and gave us rain from heaven, and fruitful seasons, filling our hearts with food and gladness.' ¹⁸And with these sayings scarce restrained they the people, that

they had not done sacrifice unto them.

¹⁹And there came thither certain Jews from Antioch and Iconium, who persuaded the people, and, having stoned Paul, drew him out of the city, supposing he had been dead. ²⁰Howbeit, as the disciples stood round about him, he rose up, and came into the city: and the next day he departed with Barnabas to Derbe. ²¹And when they had preached the gospel to that city, and had taught many, they returned again to Lystra, and to Iconium, and Antioch, ²²confirming the souls of the disciples, and exhorting them to continue in the faith, and that we must through much tribulation enter into the kingdom of God. ²³And when they had ordained them elders in every church, and had prayed with fasting, they commended them to the Lord, on whom they believed. ²⁴And after they had passed throughout Pisidia, they came to Pamphylia. ²⁵And when they had preached the word in Perga, they went down into Attalia, ²⁶and thence sailed to Antioch, from whence they had been recommended to the grace of God for the work which they fulfilled. ²⁷And when they were come, and had gathered the church together, they rehearsed all that God had done with them, and how he had opened the door of faith unto the Gentiles. ²⁸And there they abode long time with the disciples.

15 And certain men which came down from Judaea taught the brethren, and said, 'Except ye be circumcised after the manner of Moses, ye cannot be saved.' ²When therefore Paul and Barnabas had no small dissension and disputation with them, they determined that Paul and

Barnabas, and certain other of them, should go up to Jerusalem unto the apostles and elders about this question. ³And being brought on their way by the church, they passed through Phenice and Samaria, declaring the conversion of the Gentiles: and they caused great joy unto all the brethren. ⁴And when they were come to Jerusalem, they were received of the church, and of the apostles and elders, and they declared all things that God had done with them. ⁵ But there rose up certain of the sect of the Pharisees which believed, saying, 'That it was needful to circumcise them, and to command them to keep the law of Moses.'

⁶And the apostles and elders came together for to consider of this matter. ⁷And when there had been much disputing, Peter rose up, and said unto them, 'Men and brethren, ye know how that a good while ago God made choice among us, that the Gentiles by my mouth should hear the word of the gospel, and believe. ⁸And God, which knoweth the hearts, bare them witness, giving them the Holy Ghost, even as he did unto us; ⁹and put no difference between us and them, purifying their hearts by faith. ¹⁰Now therefore why tempt ye God, to put a yoke upon the neck of the disciples, which neither our fathers nor we were able to bear? ¹¹But we believe that through the grace of the Lord Jesus Christ we shall be saved, even as they.'

¹²Then all the multitude kept silence, and gave audience to Barnabas and Paul, declaring what miracles and wonders God had wrought among the Gentiles by them.

¹³And after they had held their peace, James answered, saying, 'Men and brethren, hearken unto me: ¹⁴Simeon hath

declared how God at the first did visit the Gentiles, to take out of them a people for his name. [15]And to this agree the words of the prophets; as it is written, [16]"After this I will return, and will build again the tabernacle of David, which is fallen down; and I will build again the ruins thereof, and I will set it up, [17]that the residue of men might seek after the Lord, and all the Gentiles, upon whom my name is called, saith the Lord, who doeth all these things. [18]Known unto God are all his works from the beginning of the world." [19]Wherefore my sentence is, that we trouble not them, which from among the Gentiles are turned to God, [20]but that we write unto them, that they abstain from pollutions of idols, and from fornication, and from things strangled, and from blood. [21]For Moses of old time hath in every city them that preach him, being read in the synagogues every sabbath day.' [22]Then pleased it the apostles and elders, with the whole church, to send chosen men of their own company to Antioch with Paul and Barnabas; namely, Judas surnamed Barsabas, and Silas, chief men among the brethren; [23]and they wrote letters by them after this manner:

'The apostles and elders and brethren send greeting unto the brethren which are of the Gentiles in Antioch and Syria and Cilicia: [24]forasmuch as we have heard, that certain which went out from us have troubled you with words, subverting your souls, saying, "Ye must be circumcised, and keep the law"; to whom we gave no such commandment; [25]it seemed good unto us, being assembled with one accord, to send chosen men unto you with our beloved Barnabas and Paul, 26 men that have hazarded their lives for the name of our Lord Jesus Christ. 27 We have sent therefore Judas and Silas, who shall also tell you the same things by mouth. 28 For it seemed good to the Holy Ghost, and to us, to lay upon you no greater burden than these necessary things, 29 that ye abstain from meats offered to idols, and from blood, and from things strangled, and from fornication, from which if ye keep yourselves, ye shall do well. Fare ye well.'

30 So when they were dismissed, they came to Antioch: and when they had gathered the multitude together, they delivered the epistle, 31 which when they had read, they rejoiced for the consolation. 32 And Judas and Silas, being prophets also themselves, exhorted the brethren with many words, and confirmed them. 33 And after they had tarried there a space, they were let go in peace from the brethren unto the apostles. 34 Notwithstanding it pleased Silas to abide there still. 35 Paul also and Barnabas continued in Antioch, teaching and preaching the word of the Lord, with many others also.

36 And some days after Paul said unto Barnabas, 'Let us go again and visit our brethren in every city where we have preached the word of the Lord, and see how they do.' 37 And Barnabas determined to take with them John, whose surname was Mark. 38 But Paul thought not good to take him with them, who departed from them from Pamphylia, and

went not with them to the work. ³⁹ And the contention was so sharp between them, that they departed asunder one from the other: and so Barnabas took Mark, and sailed unto Cyprus; ⁴⁰ and Paul chose Silas, and departed, being recommended by the brethren unto the grace of God. ⁴¹ And he went through Syria and Cilicia, confirming the churches.

16 Then came he to Derbe and Lystra: and, behold, a certain disciple was there, named Timotheus, the son of a certain woman, which was a Jewess, and believed; but his father was a Greek, ² which was well reported of by the brethren that were at Lystra and Iconium. ³ Him would Paul have to go forth with him; and took and circumcised him because of the Jews which were in those quarters; for they knew all that his father was a Greek. ⁴ And as they went through the cities, they delivered them the decrees for to keep, that were ordained of the apostles and elders which were at Jerusalem. ⁵ And so were the churches established in the faith, and increased in number daily. ⁶ Now when they had gone throughout Phrygia and the region of Galatia, and were forbidden of the Holy Ghost to preach the word in Asia, ⁷ after they were come to Mysia, they assayed to go into Bithynia; but the Spirit suffered them not. ⁸ And they passing by Mysia came down to Troas. ⁹ And a vision appeared to Paul in the night: there stood a man of Macedonia, and prayed him, saying, 'Come over into Macedonia, and help us.' ¹⁰ And after he had seen the vision, immediately we endeavoured to go into Macedonia, assuredly gathering that the Lord had called us for to preach the gospel unto them. ¹¹Therefore loosing from Troas, we came with a straight course to Samothracia, and the next day to Neapolis; ¹²and from thence to Philippi, which is the chief city of that part of Macedonia, and a colony; and we were in that city abiding certain days. ¹³And on the sabbath we went out of the city by a river side, where prayer was wont to be made; and we sat down, and spake unto the women which resorted thither.

¹⁴And a certain woman named Lydia, a seller of purple, of the city of Thyatira, which worshipped God, heard us, whose heart the Lord opened, that she attended unto the things which were spoken of Paul. ¹⁵And when she was baptized, and her household, she besought us, saying, 'If ye have judged me to be faithful to the Lord, come into my house, and abide there.' And she constrained us.

¹⁶And it came to pass, as we went to prayer, a certain damsel possessed with a spirit of divination met us, which brought her masters much gain by soothsaying. ¹⁷The same followed Paul and us, and cried, saying, 'These men are the servants of the most high God, which shew unto us the way of salvation.' ¹⁸And this did she many days. But Paul, being grieved, turned and said to the spirit, 'I command thee in the name of Jesus Christ to come out of her.' And he came out the same hour.

¹⁹And when her masters saw that the hope of their gains was gone, they caught Paul and Silas, and drew them into the marketplace unto the rulers, ²⁰and brought them to the magistrates, saying, 'These men, being Jews, do exceedingly trouble our city, ²¹and teach customs, which are not lawful

for us to receive, neither to observe, being Romans.' ²²And the multitude rose up together against them: and the magistrates rent off their clothes, and commanded to beat them. ²³And when they had laid many stripes upon them, they cast them into prison, charging the jailor to keep them safely, ²⁴who, having received such a charge, thrust them into the inner prison, and made their feet fast in the stocks.

²⁵And at midnight Paul and Silas prayed, and sang praises unto God: and the prisoners heard them. ²⁶And suddenly there was a great earthquake, so that the foundations of the prison were shaken: and immediately all the doors were opened, and every one's bands were loosed. ²⁷And the keeper of the prison awaking out of his sleep, and seeing the prison doors open, he drew out his sword, and would have killed himself, supposing that the prisoners had been fled. ²⁸But Paul cried with a loud voice, saying, 'Do thyself no harm: for we are all here.' ²⁹Then he called for a light, and sprang in, and came trembling, and fell down before Paul and Silas, ³⁰and brought them out, and said, 'Sirs, what must I do to be saved?' ³¹And they said, 'Believe on the Lord Jesus Christ, and thou shalt be saved, and thy house.' ³²And they spake unto him the word of the Lord, and to all that were in his house. ³³And he took them the same hour of the night, and washed their stripes; and was baptized, he and all his, straightway. ³⁴And when he had brought them into his house, he set meat before them, and rejoiced, believing in God with all his house. ³⁵And when it was day, the magistrates sent the serjeants, saying, 'Let those men go.' ³⁶And the keeper of the prison told this saying to Paul, 'The magis-

trates have sent to let you go: now therefore depart, and go in peace.' ³⁷ But Paul said unto them, 'They have beaten us openly uncondemned, being Romans, and have cast us into prison; and now do they thrust us out privily? Nay verily; but let them come themselves and fetch us out.' ³⁸And the serjeants told these words unto the magistrates: and they feared, when they heard that they were Romans. ³⁹And they came and besought them, and brought them out, and desired them to depart out of the city. ⁴⁰And they went out of the prison, and entered into the house of Lydia: and when they had seen the brethren, they comforted them, and departed.

17 Now when they had passed through Amphipolis and Apollonia, they came to Thessalonica, where was a synagogue of the Jews. ²And Paul, as his manner was, went in unto them, and three sabbath days reasoned with them out of the scriptures, ³opening and alleging, that Christ must needs have suffered, and risen again from the dead; and that this Jesus, whom I preach unto you, is Christ. ⁴And some of them believed, and consorted with Paul and Silas; and of the devout Greeks a great multitude, and of the chief women not a few.

⁵But the Jews which believed not, moved with envy, took unto them certain lewd fellows of the baser sort, and gathered a company, and set all the city on an uproar, and assaulted the house of Jason, and sought to bring them out to the people. ⁶And when they found them not, they drew Jason and certain brethren unto the rulers of the city, crying, 'These

that have turned the world upside down are come hither also, ⁷whom Jason hath received: and these all do contrary to the decrees of Caesar, saying that there is another king, one Jesus.' ⁸And they troubled the people and the rulers of the city, when they heard these things. ⁹And when they had taken security of Jason, and of the other, they let them go.

¹⁰And the brethren immediately sent away Paul and Silas by night unto Berea, who coming thither went into the synagogue of the Jews. ¹¹These were more noble than those in Thessalonica, in that they received the word with all readiness of mind, and searched the scriptures daily, whether those things were so. ¹²Therefore many of them believed; also of honourable women which were Greeks, and of men, not a few. ¹³But when the Jews of Thessalonica had knowledge that the word of God was preached of Paul at Berea, they came thither also, and stirred up the people. ¹⁴And then immediately the brethren sent away Paul to go as it were to the sea, but Silas and Timotheus abode there still. ¹⁵And they that conducted Paul brought him unto Athens; and receiving a commandment unto Silas and Timotheus for to come to him with all speed, they departed.

¹⁶Now while Paul waited for them at Athens, his spirit was stirred in him, when he saw the city wholly given to idolatry. ¹⁷Therefore disputed he in the synagogue with the Jews, and with the devout persons, and in the market daily with them that met with him. ¹⁸Then certain philosophers of the Epicureans, and of the Stoicks, encountered him. And some said, 'What will this babbler say?' Other some, 'He seemeth to be a setter forth of strange gods': because he

preached unto them Jesus, and the resurrection. ¹⁹And they took him, and brought him unto Areopagus, saying, 'May we know what this new doctrine, whereof thou speakest, is? ²⁰For thou bringest certain strange things to our ears: we would know therefore what these things mean.' ²¹(For all the Athenians and strangers which were there spent their time in nothing else, but either to tell, or to hear some new thing.)

²²Then Paul stood in the midst of Mars' hill, and said, 'Ye men of Athens, I perceive that in all things ye are too superstitious. ²³For as I passed by, and beheld your devotions, I found an altar with this inscription, "To the unknown god". Whom therefore ye ignorantly worship, him declare I unto you. ²⁴God that made the world and all things therein, seeing that he is Lord of heaven and earth, dwelleth not in temples made with hands; ²⁵neither is worshipped with men's hands, as though he needed any thing, seeing he giveth to all life, and breath, and all things; ²⁶and hath made of one blood all nations of men for to dwell on all the face of the earth, and hath determined the times before appointed, and the bounds of their habitation; ²⁷that they should seek the Lord, if haply they might feel after him, and find him, though he be not far from every one of us, ²⁸for in him we live, and move, and have our being; as certain also of your own poets have said, "For we are also his offspring." ²⁹Forasmuch then as we are the offspring of God, we ought not to think that the Godhead is like unto gold, or silver, or stone, graven by art and man's device. ³⁰And the times of this ignorance God winked at; but now commandeth all men every where to repent, ³¹because he hath appointed a day, in the which he

will judge the world in righteousness by that man whom he hath ordained; whereof he hath given assurance unto all men, in that he hath raised him from the dead.'

³²And when they heard of the resurrection of the dead, some mocked, and others said, 'We will hear thee again of this matter.' ³³So Paul departed from among them. ³⁴Howbeit certain men clave unto him, and believed: among the which was Dionysius the Areopagite, and a woman named Damaris, and others with them.

18 After these things Paul departed from Athens, and came to Corinth; ²and found a certain Jew named Aquila, born in Pontus, lately come from Italy, with his wife Priscilla (because that Claudius had commanded all Jews to depart from Rome), and came unto them. ³And because he was of the same craft, he abode with them, and wrought, for by their occupation they were tentmakers. ⁴And he reasoned in the synagogue every sabbath, and persuaded the Jews and the Greeks. ⁵And when Silas and Timotheus were come from Macedonia, Paul was pressed in the spirit, and testified to the Jews that Jesus was Christ. ⁶And when they opposed themselves, and blasphemed, he shook his raiment, and said unto them, 'Your blood be upon your own heads; I am clean: from henceforth I will go unto the Gentiles.'

⁷And he departed thence, and entered into a certain man's house, named Justus, one that worshipped God, whose house joined hard to the synagogue. ⁸And Crispus, the chief ruler of the synagogue, believed on the Lord with all his house; and many of the Corinthians hearing believed, and

were baptized. ⁹Then spake the Lord to Paul in the night by a vision, 'Be not afraid, but speak, and hold not thy peace, ¹⁰for I am with thee, and no man shall set on thee to hurt thee, for I have much people in this city.' ¹¹And he continued there a year and six months, teaching the word of God among them.

¹²And when Gallio was the deputy of Achaia, the Jews made insurrection with one accord against Paul, and brought him to the judgment seat, ¹³saying, 'This fellow persuadeth men to worship God contrary to the law.' ¹⁴And when Paul was now about to open his mouth, Gallio said unto the Jews, 'If it were a matter of wrong or wicked lewdness, O ye Jews, reason would that I should bear with you, ¹⁵but if it be a question of words and names, and of your law, look ye to it; for I will be no judge of such matters.' ¹⁶And he drave them from the judgment seat. ¹⁷Then all the Greeks took Sosthenes, the chief ruler of the synagogue, and beat him before the judgment seat. And Gallio cared for none of those things.

¹⁸And Paul after this tarried there yet a good while, and then took his leave of the brethren, and sailed thence into Syria, and with him Priscilla and Aquila; having shorn his head in Cenchrea; for he had a vow. ¹⁹And he came to Ephesus, and left them there, but he himself entered into the synagogue, and reasoned with the Jews. ²⁰When they desired him to tarry longer time with them, he consented not, ²¹but bade them farewell, saying, 'I must by all means keep this feast that cometh in Jerusalem, but I will return again unto you, if God will.' And he sailed from Ephesus.

²²And when he had landed at Caesarea, and gone up, and saluted the church, he went down to Antioch. ²³And after he had spent some time there, he departed, and went over all the country of Galatia and Phrygia in order, strengthening all the disciples.

²⁴And a certain Jew named Apollos, born at Alexandria, an eloquent man, and mighty in the scriptures, came to Ephesus. ²⁵This man was instructed in the way of the Lord; and being fervent in the spirit, he spake and taught diligently the things of the Lord, knowing only the baptism of John. ²⁶And he began to speak boldly in the synagogue, whom when Aquila and Priscilla had heard, they took him unto them, and expounded unto him the way of God more perfectly. ²⁷And when he was disposed to pass into Achaia, the brethren wrote, exhorting the disciples to receive him, who, when he was come, helped them much which had believed through grace; ²⁸for he mightily convinced the Jews, and that publickly, shewing by the scriptures that Jesus was Christ.

19 And it came to pass, that, while Apollos was at Corinth, Paul having passed through the upper coasts came to Ephesus: and finding certain disciples, ²he said unto them, 'Have ye received the Holy Ghost since ye believed?' And they said unto him, 'We have not so much as heard whether there be any Holy Ghost.' ³And he said unto them, 'Unto what then were ye baptized?' And they said, 'Unto John's baptism.' ⁴Then said Paul, John verily baptized with the baptism of repentance, saying unto the people, that they

should believe on him which should come after him, that is, on Christ Jesus. ⁵When they heard this, they were baptized in the name of the Lord Jesus. ⁶And when Paul had laid his hands upon them, the Holy Ghost came on them; and they spake with tongues, and prophesied. ⁷And all the men were about twelve. ⁸And he went into the synagogue, and spake boldly for the space of three months, disputing and persuading the things concerning the kingdom of God. ⁹But when divers were hardened, and believed not, but spake evil of that way before the multitude, he departed from them, and separated the disciples, disputing daily in the school of one Tyrannus. ¹⁰And this continued by the space of two years; so that all they which dwelt in Asia heard the word of the Lord Jesus, both Jews and Greeks. ¹¹And God wrought special miracles by the hands of Paul, ¹²so that from his body were brought unto the sick handkerchiefs or aprons, and the diseases departed from them, and the evil spirits went out of them.

¹³Then certain of the vagabond Jews, exorcists, took upon them to call over them which had evil spirits the name of the Lord Jesus, saying, 'We adjure you by Jesus whom Paul preacheth.' ¹⁴And there were seven sons of one Sceva, a Jew, and chief of the priests, which did so. ¹⁵And the evil spirit answered and said, 'Jesus I know, and Paul I know; but who are ye?' ¹⁶And the man in whom the evil spirit was leaped on them, and overcame them, and prevailed against them, so that they fled out of that house naked and wounded. ¹⁷And this was known to all the Jews and Greeks also dwelling at Ephesus; and fear fell on them all, and the name of the Lord

Jesus was magnified. ¹⁸And many that believed came, and confessed, and shewed their deeds. ¹⁹Many of them also which used curious arts brought their books together, and burned them before all men; and they counted the price of them, and found it fifty thousand pieces of silver. ²⁰So mightily grew the word of God and prevailed.

²¹After these things were ended, Paul purposed in the spirit, when he had passed through Macedonia and Achaia, to go to Jerusalem, saying, 'After I have been there, I must also see Rome.' ²²So he sent into Macedonia two of them that ministered unto him, Timotheus and Erastus; but he himself stayed in Asia for a season. ²³And the same time there arose no small stir about that way. ²⁴For a certain man named Demetrius, a silversmith, which made silver shrines for Diana, brought no small gain unto the craftsmen, ²⁵ whom he called together with the workmen of like occupation, and said, 'Sirs, ye know that by this craft we have our wealth. ²⁶Moreover ye see and hear, that not alone at Ephesus, but almost throughout all Asia, this Paul hath persuaded and turned away much people, saying that they be no gods, which are made with hands; ²⁷so that not only this our craft is in danger to be set at nought; but also that the temple of the great goddess Diana should be despised, and her magnificence should be destroyed, whom all Asia and the world worshippeth.' ²⁸And when they heard these sayings, they were full of wrath, and cried out, saying, 'Great is Diana of the Ephesians.' ²⁹And the whole city was filled with confusion: and having caught Gaius and Aristarchus, men of Macedonia, Paul's companions in travel, they rushed with

one accord into the theatre. ³⁰And when Paul would have entered in unto the people, the disciples suffered him not. ³¹And certain of the chief of Asia, which were his friends, sent unto him, desiring him that he would not adventure himself into the theatre. ³²Some therefore cried one thing, and some another, for the assembly was confused; and the more part knew not wherefore they were come together. ³³And they drew Alexander out of the multitude, the Jews putting him forward. And Alexander beckoned with the hand, and would have made his defence unto the people. ³⁴But when they knew that he was a Jew, all with one voice about the space of two hours cried out, 'Great is Diana of the Ephesians.' ³⁵And when the townclerk had appeased the people, he said, 'Ye men of Ephesus, what man is there that knoweth not how that the city of the Ephesians is a worshipper of the great goddess Diana, and of the image which fell down from Jupiter? ³⁶Seeing then that these things cannot be spoken against, ye ought to be quiet, and to do nothing rashly. ³⁷For ye have brought hither these men, which are neither robbers of churches, nor yet blasphemers of your goddess. ³⁸Wherefore if Demetrius, and the craftsmen which are with him, have a matter against any man, the law is open, and there are deputies: let them implead one another. ³⁹But if ye enquire any thing concerning other matters, it shall be determined in a lawful assembly. ⁴⁰For we are in danger to be called in question for this day's uproar, there being no cause whereby we may give an account of this concourse.' ⁴¹And when he had thus spoken, he dismissed the assembly.

20 And after the uproar was ceased, Paul called unto him the disciples, and embraced them, and departed for to go into Macedonia. ²And when he had gone over those parts, and had given them much exhortation, he came into Greece, ³and there abode three months. And when the Jews laid wait for him, as he was about to sail into Syria, he purposed to return through Macedonia. ⁴And there accompanied him into Asia Sopater of Berea; and of the Thessalonians, Aristarchus and Secundus; and Gaius of Derbe, and Timotheus; and of Asia, Tychicus and Trophimus. ⁵These going before tarried for us at Troas. ⁶And we sailed away from Philippi after the days of unleavened bread, and came unto them to Troas in five days; where we abode seven days. ⁷And upon the first day of the week, when the disciples came together to break bread, Paul preached unto them, ready to depart on the morrow; and continued his speech until midnight. ⁸And there were many lights in the upper chamber, where they were gathered together. ⁹And there sat in a window a certain young man named Eutychus, being fallen into a deep sleep: and as Paul was long preaching, he sunk down with sleep, and fell down from the third loft, and was taken up dead. ¹⁰And Paul went down, and fell on him, and embracing him said, 'Trouble not yourselves; for his life is in him.' ¹¹When he therefore was come up again, and had broken bread, and eaten, and talked a long while, even till break of day, so he departed. ¹²And they brought the young man alive, and were not a little comforted.

¹³And we went before to ship, and sailed unto Assos, there intending to take in Paul, for so had he appointed,

minding himself to go afoot. ¹⁴And when he met with us at Assos, we took him in, and came to Mitylene. ¹⁵And we sailed thence, and came the next day over against Chios; and the next day we arrived at Samos, and tarried at Trogyllium; and the next day we came to Miletus. ¹⁶For Paul had determined to sail by Ephesus, because he would not spend the time in Asia; for he hasted, if it were possible for him, to be at Jerusalem the day of Pentecost.

¹⁷And from Miletus he sent to Ephesus, and called the elders of the church. ¹⁸And when they were come to him, he said unto them, 'Ye know, from the first day that I came into Asia, after what manner I have been with you at all seasons, ¹⁹serving the Lord with all humility of mind, and with many tears, and temptations, which befell me by the lying in wait of the Jews; ²⁰and how I kept back nothing that was profitable unto you, but have shewed you, and have taught you publickly, and from house to house, ²¹testifying both to the Jews, and also to the Greeks, repentance toward God, and faith toward our Lord Jesus Christ. ²²And now, behold, I go bound in the spirit unto Jerusalem, not knowing the things that shall befall me there: ²³save that the Holy Ghost witnesseth in every city, saying that bonds and afflictions abide me. ²⁴But none of these things move me, neither count I my life dear unto myself, so that I might finish my course with joy, and the ministry, which I have received of the Lord Jesus, to testify the gospel of the grace of God. ²⁵And now, behold, I know that ye all, among whom I have gone preaching the kingdom of God, shall see my face no more. ²⁶Wherefore I take you to record this day, that I am pure from the blood of

all men. [27] For I have not shunned to declare unto you all the counsel of God.

[28] 'Take heed therefore unto yourselves, and to all the flock, over the which the Holy Ghost hath made you overseers, to feed the church of God, which he hath purchased with his own blood. [29] For I know this, that after my departing shall grievous wolves enter in among you, not sparing the flock. [30] Also of your own selves shall men arise, speaking perverse things, to draw away disciples after them. [31] Therefore watch, and remember, that by the space of three years I ceased not to warn every one night and day with tears. [32] And now, brethren, I commend you to God, and to the word of his grace, which is able to build you up, and to give you an inheritance among all them which are sanctified. [33] I have coveted no man's silver, or gold, or apparel. [34] Yea, ye yourselves know, that these hands have ministered unto my necessities, and to them that were with me. [35] I have shewed you all things, how that so labouring ye ought to support the weak, and to remember the words of the Lord Jesus, how he said, "It is more blessed to give than to receive."'

[36] And when he had thus spoken, he kneeled down, and prayed with them all. [37] And they all wept sore, and fell on Paul's neck, and kissed him, [38] sorrowing most of all for the words which he spake, that they should see his face no more. And they accompanied him unto the ship.

21 And it came to pass, that after we were gotten from them, and had launched, we came with a straight course unto Coos, and the day following unto Rhodes, and

from thence unto Patara. ²And finding a ship sailing over unto Phenicia, we went aboard, and set forth. ³Now when we had discovered Cyprus, we left it on the left hand, and sailed into Syria, and landed at Tyre, for there the ship was to unlade her burden. ⁴And finding disciples, we tarried there seven days, who said to Paul through the Spirit, that he should not go up to Jerusalem. ⁵And when we had accomplished those days, we departed and went our way; and they all brought us on our way, with wives and children, till we were out of the city; and we kneeled down on the shore, and prayed. ⁶And when we had taken our leave one of another, we took ship; and they returned home again.

⁷And when we had finished our course from Tyre, we came to Ptolemais, and saluted the brethren, and abode with them one day. ⁸And the next day we that were of Paul's company departed, and came unto Caesarea; and we entered into the house of Philip the evangelist, which was one of the seven; and abode with him. ⁹And the same man had four daughters, virgins, which did prophesy. ¹⁰And as we tarried there many days, there came down from Judaea a certain prophet, named Agabus. ¹¹And when he was come unto us, he took Paul's girdle, and bound his own hands and feet, and said, 'Thus saith the Holy Ghost, "So shall the Jews at Jerusalem bind the man that owneth this girdle, and shall deliver him into the hands of the Gentiles."' ¹²And when we heard these things, both we, and they of that place, besought him not to go up to Jerusalem. ¹³Then Paul answered, 'What mean ye to weep and to break mine heart? For I am ready not to be bound only, but also to die at Jerusalem for the

name of the Lord Jesus.' ¹⁴And when he would not be persuaded, we ceased, saying, 'The will of the Lord be done.'

¹⁵And after those days we took up our carriages, and
went up to Jerusalem. ¹⁶There went with us also certain of
the disciples of Caesarea, and brought with them one Mna-
son of Cyprus, an old disciple, with whom we should lodge.

¹⁷And when we were come to Jerusalem, the brethren
received us gladly. ¹⁸And the day following Paul went in
with us unto James; and all the elders were present. ¹⁹And
when he had saluted them, he declared particularly what
things God had wrought among the Gentiles by his ministry. ²⁰And when they heard it, they glorified the Lord, and
said unto him, 'Thou seest, brother, how many thousands of
Jews there are which believe; and they are all zealous of the
law; ²¹and they are informed of thee, that thou teachest all
the Jews which are among the Gentiles to forsake Moses,
saying that they ought not to circumcise their children, neither to walk after the customs. ²²What is it therefore? The
multitude must needs come together, for they will hear that
thou art come. ²³Do therefore this that we say to thee: we
have four men which have a vow on them; ²⁴them take, and
purify thyself with them, and be at charges with them, that
they may shave their heads; and all may know that those
things, whereof they were informed concerning thee, are
nothing; but that thou thyself also walkest orderly, and
keepest the law. ²⁵As touching the Gentiles which believe,
we have written and concluded that they observe no such
thing, save only that they keep themselves from things
offered to idols, and from blood, and from strangled, and

from fornication.' ²⁶ Then Paul took the men, and the next day purifying himself with them entered into the temple, to signify the accomplishment of the days of purification, until that an offering should be offered for every one of them.

²⁷And when the seven days were almost ended, the Jews which were of Asia, when they saw him in the temple, stirred up all the people, and laid hands on him, ²⁸crying out, 'Men of Israel, help: this is the man, that teacheth all men every where against the people, and the law, and this place; and further brought Greeks also into the temple, and hath polluted this holy place.' ²⁹(For they had seen before with him in the city Trophimus an Ephesian, whom they supposed that Paul had brought into the temple.) ³⁰And all the city was moved, and the people ran together; and they took Paul, and drew him out of the temple; and forthwith the doors were shut. ³¹And as they went about to kill him, tidings came unto the chief captain of the band, that all Jerusalem was in an uproar. ³² Who immediately took soldiers and centurions, and ran down unto them: and when they saw the chief captain and the soldiers, they left beating of Paul. ³³ Then the chief captain came near, and took him, and commanded him to be bound with two chains; and demanded who he was, and what he had done. ³⁴And some cried one thing, some another, among the multitude: and when he could not know the certainty for the tumult, he commanded him to be carried into the castle. ³⁵And when he came upon the stairs, so it was, that he was borne of the soldiers for the violence of the people. ³⁶ For the multitude of the people followed after, crying, 'Away with him.'

³⁷And as Paul was to be led into the castle, he said unto the chief captain, 'May I speak unto thee?' Who said, 'Canst thou speak Greek? ³⁸Art not thou that Egyptian, which before these days madest an uproar, and leddest out into the wilderness four thousand men that were murderers?' ³⁹But Paul said, 'I am a man which am a Jew of Tarsus, a city in Cilicia, a citizen of no mean city: and, I beseech thee, suffer me to speak unto the people.' ⁴⁰And when he had given him licence, Paul stood on the stairs, and beckoned with the hand unto the people. And when there was made a great silence, he spake unto them in the Hebrew tongue, saying,

22 'Men, brethren, and fathers, hear ye my defence which I make now unto you.' ²(And when they heard that he spake in the Hebrew tongue to them, they kept the more silence: and he saith,) ³'I am verily a man which am a Jew, born in Tarsus, a city in Cilicia, yet brought up in this city at the feet of Gamaliel, and taught according to the perfect manner of the law of the fathers, and was zealous toward God, as ye all are this day. ⁴And I persecuted this way unto the death, binding and delivering into prisons both men and women. ⁵As also the high priest doth bear me witness, and all the estate of the elders, from whom also I received letters unto the brethren, and went to Damascus, to bring them which were there bound unto Jerusalem, for to be punished.

⁶'And it came to pass, that, as I made my journey, and was come nigh unto Damascus about noon, suddenly there shone from heaven a great light round about me. ⁷And I fell

unto the ground, and heard a voice saying unto me, "Saul, Saul, why persecutest thou me?" [8]And I answered, "Who art thou, Lord?" And he said unto me, "I am Jesus of Nazareth, whom thou persecutest." [9]And they that were with me saw indeed the light, and were afraid; but they heard not the voice of him that spake to me. [10]And I said, "What shall I do, Lord?" And the Lord said unto me, "Arise, and go into Damascus; and there it shall be told thee of all things which are appointed for thee to do." [11]And when I could not see for the glory of that light, being led by the hand of them that were with me, I came into Damascus.

[12]'And one Ananias, a devout man according to the law, having a good report of all the Jews which dwelt there, [13]came unto me, and stood, and said unto me, "Brother Saul, receive thy sight." And the same hour I looked up upon him. [14]And he said, "The God of our fathers hath chosen thee, that thou shouldest know his will, and see that Just One, and shouldest hear the voice of his mouth. [15]For thou shalt be his witness unto all men of what thou hast seen and heard. [16]And now why tarriest thou? Arise, and be baptized, and wash away thy sins, calling on the name of the Lord."

[17]'And it came to pass, that, when I was come again to Jerusalem, even while I prayed in the temple, I was in a trance; [18]and saw him saying unto me, "Make haste, and get thee quickly out of Jerusalem, for they will not receive thy testimony concerning me." [19]And I said, "Lord, they know that I imprisoned and beat in every synagogue them that believed on thee: [20]and when the blood of thy martyr

Stephen was shed, I also was standing by, and consenting unto his death, and kept the raiment of them that slew him." ²¹And he said unto me, "Depart: for I will send thee far hence unto the Gentiles."'

²²And they gave him audience unto this word, and then lifted up their voices, and said, 'Away with such a fellow from the earth, for it is not fit that he should live.' ²³And as they cried out, and cast off their clothes, and threw dust into the air, ²⁴ the chief captain commanded him to be brought into the castle, and bade that he should be examined by scourging; that he might know wherefore they cried so against him. ²⁵And as they bound him with thongs, Paul said unto the centurion that stood by, 'Is it lawful for you to scourge a man that is a Roman, and uncondemned?' ²⁶ When the centurion heard that, he went and told the chief captain, saying, 'Take heed what thou doest, for this man is a Roman.' ²⁷ Then the chief captain came, and said unto him, 'Tell me, art thou a Roman?' He said, 'Yea.' ²⁸And the chief captain answered, 'With a great sum obtained I this freedom.' And Paul said, 'But I was free born.' ²⁹ Then straightway they departed from him which should have examined him: and the chief captain also was afraid, after he knew that he was a Roman, and because he had bound him.

³⁰ On the morrow, because he would have known the certainty wherefore he was accused of the Jews, he loosed him from his bands, and commanded the chief priests and all their council to appear, and brought Paul down, and set him before them.

23 And Paul, earnestly beholding the council, said, 'Men and brethren, I have lived in all good conscience before God until this day.' ²And the high priest Ananias commanded them that stood by him to smite him on the mouth. ³Then said Paul unto him, 'God shall smite thee, thou whited wall, for sittest thou to judge me after the law, and commandest me to be smitten contrary to the law?' ⁴And they that stood by said, 'Revilest thou God's high priest?' ⁵Then said Paul, 'I wist not, brethren, that he was the high priest, for it is written, "Thou shalt not speak evil of the ruler of thy people."'

⁶But when Paul perceived that the one part were Sadducees, and the other Pharisees, he cried out in the council, 'Men and brethren, I am a Pharisee, the son of a Pharisee: of the hope and resurrection of the dead I am called in question.' ⁷And when he had so said, there arose a dissension between the Pharisees and the Sadducees: and the multitude was divided. ⁸For the Sadducees say that there is no resurrection, neither angel, nor spirit; but the Pharisees confess both. ⁹And there arose a great cry; and the scribes that were of the Pharisees' part arose, and strove, saying, 'We find no evil in this man; but if a spirit or an angel hath spoken to him, let us not fight against God.' ¹⁰And when there arose a great dissension, the chief captain, fearing lest Paul should have been pulled in pieces of them, commanded the soldiers to go down, and to take him by force from among them, and to bring him into the castle.

¹¹And the night following the Lord stood by him, and said, 'Be of good cheer, Paul, for as thou hast testified of me

in Jerusalem, so must thou bear witness also at Rome.'

¹²And when it was day, certain of the Jews banded together, and bound themselves under a curse, saying that they would neither eat nor drink till they had killed Paul. ¹³And they were more than forty which had made this conspiracy. ¹⁴And they came to the chief priests and elders, and said, 'We have bound ourselves under a great curse, that we will eat nothing until we have slain Paul. ¹⁵Now therefore ye with the council signify to the chief captain that he bring him down unto you to morrow, as though ye would enquire something more perfectly concerning him: and we, or ever he come near, are ready to kill him.'

¹⁶And when Paul's sister's son heard of their lying in wait, he went and entered into the castle, and told Paul. ¹⁷Then Paul called one of the centurions unto him, and said, 'Bring this young man unto the chief captain, for he hath a certain thing to tell him.' ¹⁸So he took him, and brought him to the chief captain, and said, 'Paul the prisoner called me unto him, and prayed me to bring this young man unto thee, who hath something to say unto thee.' ¹⁹Then the chief captain took him by the hand, and went with him aside privately, and asked him, 'What is that thou hast to tell me?' ²⁰And he said, 'The Jews have agreed to desire thee that thou wouldest bring down Paul to morrow into the council, as though they would enquire somewhat of him more perfectly. ²¹But do not thou yield unto them, for there lie in wait for him of them more than forty men, which have bound themselves with an oath, that they will neither eat nor drink till they have killed him: and now are they ready, looking for

a promise from thee.' ²² So the chief captain then let the young man depart, and charged him, 'See thou tell no man that thou hast shewed these things to me.'

²³ And he called unto him two centurions, saying, 'Make ready two hundred soldiers to go to Caesarea, and horsemen threescore and ten, and spearmen two hundred, at the third hour of the night; ²⁴ and provide them beasts, that they may set Paul on, and bring him safe unto Felix the governor.' ²⁵ And he wrote a letter after this manner:

²⁶ 'Claudius Lysias unto the most excellent governor Felix sendeth greeting. ²⁷ This man was taken of the Jews, and should have been killed of them: then came I with an army, and rescued him, having understood that he was a Roman. ²⁸ And when I would have known the cause wherefore they accused him, I brought him forth into their council, ²⁹ whom I perceived to be accused of questions of their law, but to have nothing laid to his charge worthy of death or of bonds. ³⁰ And when it was told me how that the Jews laid wait for the man, I sent straightway to thee, and gave commandment to his accusers also to say before thee what they had against him. Farewell.'

³¹ Then the soldiers, as it was commanded them, took Paul, and brought him by night to Antipatris. ³² On the morrow they left the horsemen to go with him, and returned to the castle, ³³ who, when they came to Caesarea, and delivered the epistle to the governor, presented Paul also before

him. ³⁴And when the governor had read the letter, he asked of what province he was. And when he understood that he was of Cilicia, ³⁵ 'I will hear thee,' said he, 'when thine accusers are also come.' And he commanded him to be kept in Herod's judgment hall.

24 And after five days Ananias the high priest descended with the elders, and with a certain orator named Tertullus, who informed the governor against Paul. ²And when he was called forth, Tertullus began to accuse him, saying, 'Seeing that by thee we enjoy great quietness, and that very worthy deeds are done unto this nation by thy providence, ³ we accept it always, and in all places, most noble Felix, with all thankfulness. ⁴Notwithstanding, that I be not further tedious unto thee, I pray thee that thou wouldest hear us of thy clemency a few words. ⁵For we have found this man a pestilent fellow, and a mover of sedition among all the Jews throughout the world, and a ringleader of the sect of the Nazarenes, ⁶ who also hath gone about to profane the temple, whom we took, and would have judged according to our law. ⁷But the chief captain Lysias came upon us, and with great violence took him away out of our hands, ⁸commanding his accusers to come unto thee: by examining of whom thyself mayest take knowledge of all these things, whereof we accuse him.'

⁹And the Jews also assented, saying that these things were so.

¹⁰Then Paul, after that the governor had beckoned unto him to speak, answered, 'Forasmuch as I know that thou

hast been of many years a judge unto this nation, I do the more cheerfully answer for myself, ⁿbecause that thou mayest understand, that there are yet but twelve days since I went up to Jerusalem for to worship. ¹²And they neither found me in the temple disputing with any man, neither raising up the people, neither in the synagogues, nor in the city: ¹³neither can they prove the things whereof they now accuse me. ¹⁴But this I confess unto thee, that after the way which they call heresy, so worship I the God of my fathers, believing all things which are written in the law and in the prophets, ¹⁵and have hope toward God, which they themselves also allow, that there shall be a resurrection of the dead, both of the just and unjust. ¹⁶And herein do I exercise myself, to have always a conscience void of offence toward God, and toward men. ¹⁷Now after many years I came to bring alms to my nation, and offerings. ¹⁸Whereupon certain Jews from Asia found me purified in the temple, neither with multitude, nor with tumult. ¹⁹Who ought to have been here before thee, and object, if they had ought against me. ²⁰Or else let these same here say, if they have found any evil doing in me, while I stood before the council, ²¹except it be for this one voice, that I cried standing among them, "Touching the resurrection of the dead I am called in question by you this day."'

²²And when Felix heard these things, having more perfect knowledge of that way, he deferred them, and said, 'When Lysias the chief captain shall come down, I will know the uttermost of your matter.' ²³And he commanded a centurion to keep Paul, and to let him have liberty, and that he

should forbid none of his acquaintance to minister or come unto him. ²⁴And after certain days, when Felix came with his wife Drusilla, which was a Jewess, he sent for Paul, and heard him concerning the faith in Christ. ²⁵And as he reasoned of righteousness, temperance, and judgment to come, Felix trembled, and answered, 'Go thy way for this time; when I have a convenient season, I will call for thee.' ²⁶He hoped also that money should have been given him of Paul, that he might loose him: wherefore he sent for him the oftener, and communed with him.

²⁷But after two years Porcius Festus came into Felix' room: and Felix, willing to shew the Jews a pleasure, left Paul bound.

25 Now when Festus was come into the province, after three days he ascended from Caesarea to Jerusalem. ²Then the high priest and the chief of the Jews informed him against Paul, and besought him, ³and desired favour against him, that he would send for him to Jerusalem, laying wait in the way to kill him. ⁴But Festus answered, that Paul should be kept at Caesarea, and that he himself would depart shortly thither. ⁵'Let them therefore,' said he, 'which among you are able, go down with me, and accuse this man, if there be any wickedness in him.'

⁶And when he had tarried among them more than ten days, he went down unto Caesarea; and the next day sitting on the judgment seat commanded Paul to be brought. ⁷And when he was come, the Jews which came down from Jerusalem stood round about, and laid many and grievous

complaints against Paul, which they could not prove. ⁸ While he answered for himself, 'Neither against the law of the Jews, neither against the temple, nor yet against Caesar, have I offended any thing at all.' ⁹ But Festus, willing to do the Jews a pleasure, answered Paul, and said, 'Wilt thou go up to Jerusalem, and there be judged of these things before me?' ¹⁰ Then said Paul, 'I stand at Caesar's judgment seat, where I ought to be judged: to the Jews have I done no wrong, as thou very well knowest. ¹¹ For if I be an offender, or have committed any thing worthy of death, I refuse not to die; but if there be none of these things whereof these accuse me, no man may deliver me unto them. I appeal unto Caesar.' ¹² Then Festus, when he had conferred with the council, answered, 'Hast thou appealed unto Caesar? Unto Caesar shalt thou go.'

¹³ And after certain days king Agrippa and Bernice came unto Caesarea to salute Festus. ¹⁴ And when they had been there many days, Festus declared Paul's cause unto the king, saying, 'There is a certain man left in bonds by Felix, ¹⁵ about whom, when I was at Jerusalem, the chief priests and the elders of the Jews informed me, desiring to have judgment against him, ¹⁶ to whom I answered, "It is not the manner of the Romans to deliver any man to die, before that he which is accused have the accusers face to face, and have licence to answer for himself concerning the crime laid against him." ¹⁷ Therefore, when they were come hither, without any delay on the morrow I sat on the judgment seat, and commanded the man to be brought forth, ¹⁸ against whom when the accusers stood up, they brought none accusation of such

things as I supposed, ¹⁹ but had certain questions against him of their own superstition, and of one Jesus, which was dead, whom Paul affirmed to be alive. ²⁰And because I doubted of such manner of questions, I asked him whether he would go to Jerusalem, and there be judged of these matters. ²¹ But when Paul had appealed to be reserved unto the hearing of Augustus, I commanded him to be kept till I might send him to Caesar.' ²² Then Agrippa said unto Festus, 'I would also hear the man myself.' 'To morrow,' said he, 'thou shalt hear him.'

²³And on the morrow, when Agrippa was come, and Bernice, with great pomp, and was entered into the place of hearing, with the chief captains, and principal men of the city, at Festus' commandment Paul was brought forth. ²⁴And Festus said, 'King Agrippa, and all men which are here present with us, ye see this man, about whom all the multitude of the Jews have dealt with me, both at Jerusalem, and also here, crying that he ought not to live any longer. ²⁵ But when I found that he had committed nothing worthy of death, and that he himself hath appealed to Augustus, I have determined to send him. ²⁶ Of whom I have no certain thing to write unto my lord. Wherefore I have brought him forth before you, and specially before thee, O king Agrippa, that, after examination had, I might have somewhat to write. ²⁷ For it seemeth to me unreasonable to send a prisoner, and not withal to signify the crimes laid against him.'

26 Then Agrippa said unto Paul, 'Thou art permitted to speak for thyself.' Then Paul stretched forth the

hand, and answered for himself:

² 'I think myself happy, king Agrippa, because I shall answer for myself this day before thee touching all the things whereof I am accused of the Jews, ³ especially because I know thee to be expert in all customs and questions which are among the Jews: wherefore I beseech thee to hear me patiently.

⁴ 'My manner of life from my youth, which was at the first among mine own nation at Jerusalem, know all the Jews, ⁵ which knew me from the beginning, if they would testify, that after the most straitest sect of our religion I lived a Pharisee. ⁶ And now I stand and am judged for the hope of the promise made of God unto our fathers, ⁷ unto which promise our twelve tribes, instantly serving God day and night, hope to come. For which hope's sake, king Agrippa, I am accused of the Jews. ⁸ Why should it be thought a thing incredible with you, that God should raise the dead?

⁹ 'I verily thought with myself, that I ought to do many things contrary to the name of Jesus of Nazareth, ¹⁰ which thing I also did in Jerusalem: and many of the saints did I shut up in prison, having received authority from the chief priests; and when they were put to death, I gave my voice against them. ¹¹ And I punished them oft in every synagogue, and compelled them to blaspheme; and being exceedingly mad against them, I persecuted them even unto strange cities.

¹² 'Whereupon as I went to Damascus with authority and commission from the chief priests, ¹³ at midday, O king, I saw in the way a light from heaven, above the brightness of the sun, shining round about me and them which journeyed

with me. ¹⁴And when we were all fallen to the earth, I heard a voice speaking unto me, and saying in the Hebrew tongue, "Saul, Saul, why persecutest thou me? It is hard for thee to kick against the pricks." ¹⁵And I said, "Who art thou, Lord?" And he said, "I am Jesus whom thou persecutest. ¹⁶But rise, and stand upon thy feet, for I have appeared unto thee for this purpose, to make thee a minister and a witness both of these things which thou hast seen, and of those things in the which I will appear unto thee; ¹⁷delivering thee from the people, and from the Gentiles, unto whom now I send thee, ¹⁸to open their eyes, and to turn them from darkness to light, and from the power of Satan unto God, that they may receive forgiveness of sins, and inheritance among them which are sanctified by faith that is in me."

¹⁹'Whereupon, O king Agrippa, I was not disobedient unto the heavenly vision, ²⁰but shewed first unto them of Damascus, and at Jerusalem, and throughout all the coasts of Judaea, and then to the Gentiles, that they should repent and turn to God, and do works meet for repentance. ²¹For these causes the Jews caught me in the temple, and went about to kill me. ²²Having therefore obtained help of God, I continue unto this day, witnessing both to small and great, saying none other things than those which the prophets and Moses did say should come, ²³that Christ should suffer, and that he should be the first that should rise from the dead, and should shew light unto the people, and to the Gentiles.'

²⁴And as he thus spake for himself, Festus said with a loud voice, 'Paul, thou art beside thyself; much learning doth make thee mad.' ²⁵But he said, 'I am not mad, most

noble Festus; but speak forth the words of truth and soberness. ²⁶ For the king knoweth of these things, before whom also I speak freely, for I am persuaded that none of these things are hidden from him, for this thing was not done in a corner. ²⁷ King Agrippa, believest thou the prophets? I know that thou believest.' ²⁸ Then Agrippa said unto Paul, 'Almost thou persuadest me to be a Christian.' ²⁹ And Paul said, 'I would to God, that not only thou, but also all that hear me this day, were both almost, and altogether such as I am, except these bonds.'

³⁰ And when he had thus spoken, the king rose up, and the governor, and Bernice, and they that sat with them: ³¹ and when they were gone aside, they talked between themselves, saying, 'This man doeth nothing worthy of death or of bonds.' ³² Then said Agrippa unto Festus, 'This man might have been set at liberty, if he had not appealed unto Caesar.'

27 And when it was determined that we should sail into Italy, they delivered Paul and certain other prisoners unto one named Julius, a centurion of Augustus' band. ² And entering into a ship of Adramyttium, we launched, meaning to sail by the coasts of Asia; one Aristarchus, a Macedonian of Thessalonica, being with us. ³ And the next day we touched at Sidon. And Julius courteously entreated Paul, and gave him liberty to go unto his friends to refresh himself. ⁴ And when we had launched from thence, we sailed under Cyprus, because the winds were contrary. ⁵ And when we had sailed over the sea of Cilicia and Pamphylia, we came to Myra, a city of Lycia. ⁶ And there the centurion

found a ship of Alexandria sailing into Italy; and he put us therein. ⁷And when we had sailed slowly many days, and scarce were come over against Cnidus, the wind not suffering us, we sailed under Crete, over against Salmone; ⁸and, hardly passing it, came unto a place which is called 'The fair havens'; nigh whereunto was the city of Lasea.

⁹Now when much time was spent, and when sailing was now dangerous, because the fast was now already past, Paul admonished them, ¹⁰and said unto them, 'Sirs, I perceive that this voyage will be with hurt and much damage, not only of the lading and ship, but also of our lives.' ¹¹Nevertheless the centurion believed the master and the owner of the ship, more than those things which were spoken by Paul. ¹²And because the haven was not commodious to winter in, the more part advised to depart thence also, if by any means they might attain to Phenice, and there to winter; which is an haven of Crete, and lieth toward the south west and north west.

¹³And when the south wind blew softly, supposing that they had obtained their purpose, loosing thence, they sailed close by Crete. ¹⁴But not long after there arose against it a tempestuous wind, called Euroclydon. ¹⁵And when the ship was caught, and could not bear up into the wind, we let her drive. ¹⁶And running under a certain island which is called Clauda, we had much work to come by the boat, ¹⁷which when they had taken up, they used helps, undergirding the ship; and, fearing lest they should fall into the quicksands, strake sail, and so were driven. ¹⁸And we being exceedingly tossed with a tempest, the next day they lightened the ship;

¹⁹and the third day we cast out with our own hands the tackling of the ship. ²⁰And when neither sun nor stars in many days appeared, and no small tempest lay on us, all hope that we should be saved was then taken away.

²¹But after long abstinence Paul stood forth in the midst of them, and said, 'Sirs, ye should have hearkened unto me, and not have loosed from Crete, and to have gained this harm and loss. ²²And now I exhort you to be of good cheer, for there shall be no loss of any man's life among you, but of the ship. ²³For there stood by me this night the angel of God, whose I am, and whom I serve, ²⁴saying, "Fear not, Paul; thou must be brought before Caesar; and, lo, God hath given thee all them that sail with thee." ²⁵Wherefore, sirs, be of good cheer: for I believe God, that it shall be even as it was told me. ²⁶Howbeit we must be cast upon a certain island.'

²⁷But when the fourteenth night was come, as we were driven up and down in Adria, about midnight the shipmen deemed that they drew near to some country; ²⁸and sounded, and found it twenty fathoms; and when they had gone a little further, they sounded again, and found it fifteen fathoms. ²⁹Then fearing lest we should have fallen upon rocks, they cast four anchors out of the stern, and wished for the day. ³⁰And as the shipmen were about to flee out of the ship, when they had let down the boat into the sea, under colour as though they would have cast anchors out of the foreship, ³¹Paul said to the centurion and to the soldiers, 'Except these abide in the ship, ye cannot be saved.' ³²Then the soldiers cut off the ropes of the boat, and let her fall off.

³³And while the day was coming on, Paul besought them all to take meat, saying, 'This day is the fourteenth day that ye have tarried and continued fasting, having taken nothing. ³⁴ Wherefore I pray you to take some meat, for this is for your health, for there shall not an hair fall from the head of any of you.' ³⁵And when he had thus spoken, he took bread, and gave thanks to God in presence of them all: and when he had broken it, he began to eat. ³⁶ Then were they all of good cheer, and they also took some meat. ³⁷And we were in all in the ship two hundred threescore and sixteen souls. ³⁸And when they had eaten enough, they lightened the ship, and cast out the wheat into the sea.

³⁹And when it was day, they knew not the land, but they discovered a certain creek with a shore, into the which they were minded, if it were possible, to thrust in the ship. ⁴⁰And when they had taken up the anchors, they committed themselves unto the sea, and loosed the rudder bands, and hoised up the mainsail to the wind, and made toward shore. ⁴¹And falling into a place where two seas met, they ran the ship aground; and the forepart stuck fast, and remained unmoveable, but the hinder part was broken with the violence of the waves. ⁴²And the soldiers' counsel was to kill the prisoners, lest any of them should swim out, and escape. ⁴³ But the centurion, willing to save Paul, kept them from their purpose; and commanded that they which could swim should cast themselves first into the sea, and get to land, ⁴⁴ and the rest, some on boards, and some on broken pieces of the ship. And so it came to pass, that they escaped all safe to land.

28 And when they were escaped, then they knew that the island was called Melita. ²And the barbarous people shewed us no little kindness, for they kindled a fire, and received us every one, because of the present rain, and because of the cold. ³And when Paul had gathered a bundle of sticks, and laid them on the fire, there came a viper out of the heat, and fastened on his hand. ⁴And when the barbarians saw the venomous beast hang on his hand, they said among themselves, 'No doubt this man is a murderer, whom, though he hath escaped the sea, yet vengeance suffereth not to live.' ⁵And he shook off the beast into the fire, and felt no harm. ⁶Howbeit they looked when he should have swollen, or fallen down dead suddenly, but after they had looked a great while, and saw no harm come to him, they changed their minds, and said that he was a god.

⁷In the same quarters were possessions of the chief man of the island, whose name was Publius; who received us, and lodged us three days courteously. ⁸And it came to pass, that the father of Publius lay sick of a fever and of a bloody flux, to whom Paul entered in, and prayed, and laid his hands on him, and healed him. ⁹So when this was done, others also, which had diseases in the island, came, and were healed, ¹⁰who also honoured us with many honours; and when we departed, they laded us with such things as were necessary.

¹¹And after three months we departed in a ship of Alexandria, which had wintered in the isle, whose sign was Castor and Pollux. ¹²And landing at Syracuse, we tarried there three days. ¹³And from thence we fetched a compass,

and came to Rhegium: and after one day the south wind blew, and we came the next day to Puteoli, ¹⁴where we found brethren, and were desired to tarry with them seven days: and so we went toward Rome. ¹⁵And from thence, when the brethren heard of us, they came to meet us as far as Appii forum, and the three taverns, whom when Paul saw, he thanked God, and took courage.

¹⁶And when we came to Rome, the centurion delivered the prisoners to the captain of the guard, but Paul was suffered to dwell by himself with a soldier that kept him.

¹⁷And it came to pass that after three days Paul called the chief of the Jews together: and when they were come together, he said unto them, 'Men and brethren, though I have committed nothing against the people, or customs of our fathers, yet was I delivered prisoner from Jerusalem into the hands of the Romans, ¹⁸who, when they had examined me, would have let me go, because there was no cause of death in me. ¹⁹But when the Jews spake against it, I was constrained to appeal unto Caesar; not that I had ought to accuse my nation of. ²⁰For this cause therefore have I called for you, to see you, and to speak with you, because that for the hope of Israel I am bound with this chain.' ²¹And they said unto him, 'We neither received letters out of Judaea concerning thee, neither any of the brethren that came shewed or spake any harm of thee. ²²But we desire to hear of thee what thou thinkest, for as concerning this sect, we know that every where it is spoken against.'

²³And when they had appointed him a day, there came many to him into his lodging; to whom he expounded and

testified the kingdom of God, persuading them concerning Jesus, both out of the law of Moses, and out of the prophets, from morning till evening. ²⁴And some believed the things which were spoken, and some believed not. ²⁵And when they agreed not among themselves, they departed, after that Paul had spoken one word, 'Well spake the Holy Ghost by Esaias the prophet unto our fathers, ²⁶saying, "Go unto this people, and say: Hearing ye shall hear, and shall not understand; and seeing ye shall see, and not perceive, ²⁷for the heart of this people is waxed gross, and their ears are dull of hearing, and their eyes have they closed, lest they should see with their eyes, and hear with their ears, and understand with their heart, and should be converted, and I should heal them." ²⁸Be it known therefore unto you, that the salvation of God is sent unto the Gentiles, and that they will hear it.' ²⁹And when he had said these words, the Jews departed, and had great reasoning among themselves. ³⁰And Paul dwelt two whole years in his own hired house, and received all that came in unto him, ³¹preaching the kingdom of God, and teaching those things which concern the Lord Jesus Christ, with all confidence, no man forbidding him.